Antitrust Consent Decrees in Theory and Practice

Antitrust Consent Decrees in Theory and Practice

Why Less Is More

Richard A. Epstein

The AEI Press

Publisher for the American Enterprise Institute

WASHINGTON, D.C.

Distributed to the Trade by National Book Network, 15200 NBN Way, Blue Ridge
Summit, PA 17214. To order call toll free 1-800-462-6420 or 1-717-794-3800.
For all other inquiries please contact the AEI Press, 1150 Seventeenth Street, N.W.,
Washington, D.C. 20036 or call 1-800-862-5801.

Library of Congress Cataloging-in-Publication Data

Epstein, Richard A.
   Antitrust consent decrees in theory and practice : why less is more /
by Richard A. Epstein
   p. cm.
   Includes index.
ISBN-13: 978-0-8447-4250-2 (pbk :   paper)
ISBN-10: 0-8447-4250-3
1. Consent decrees—United States. 2. Antitrust law—United States.
   I. Title.

   KF1657.C6E67 2007
   343.73'0721—dc22

                                                        2006103249

11 10 09 08 07   1 2 3 4 5

Contents

Foreword

The antitrust consent decree is an opaque form of government regulation that operates without many of the checks and balances that constrain and shape ordinary regulatory programs.

Federal and state agencies that regulate telephone service, electric power, insurance, hospitals, and other businesses have legal authority to direct firms to raise or lower prices, offer or refrain from offering certain services, and market their services in specified ways. But to do so the regulators must run a procedural and political gauntlet. They must first announce their intentions and collect comments or conduct hearings, then rationalize their decisions in a manner consistent with the evidence and the terms of their authorizing statutes, then wait to see if a court or legislature modifies or reverses their decisions. Sometimes their proposals attract media attention and public scrutiny that bring into play interests other than those of the firms they regulate.

Antitrust consent decrees operate without gauntlets. Many antitrust cases end with a simple up or down decision and, when the decision is for the government, with a straightforward sanction—a fine, prison term, or injunction against clearly defined violations such as price-fixing. But many big cases—where the government challenges complex commercial activities (or "patterns" of activity) of major corporations—are concluded by agreements between the government and the defendant firms that specify the firms' future activities in detail; the agreements are then approved and adopted by the trial court (often with modifications) and thereby become legal decrees. The firms thereafter operate under the informal regulation of the enforcement agency (at the federal level, the Antitrust Division of the Department of Justice or the Federal Trade Commission). According to the terms of a particular decree, the firms may be asked to submit pricing, product, marketing, and other pertinent business plans to the agency lawyers for prior review and approval. The negotiations and decisions usually transpire in private, without the involvement of the court that issued the original decree. In many cases the process has continued for decades— long after an industry's structure has changed fundamentally and the conduct the government originally complained about has dissipated and been forgotten.

Both forms of regulation have problems of their own. Regulatory agencies—operating step by step under the glare of public attention— may bow to populist pressures and deny justified price increases. Consent-degree regulation—operating in private in lawyers' offices but with one side holding the cudgel of government sanctions if the dispute reaches an impasse—presents two distinctive problems. The first is cartelization and self-dealing: Firms may use the process to coordinate pricing and marketing decisions, thereby turning the purpose of antitrust on its head. The second is abuse of power: Enforcement lawyers may use the process to maintain continuing, freewheeling authority over firms and industries, thereby exercising much greater policy discretion than if they had to prepare and prove a new antitrust case.

In this highly illuminating study, Richard A. Epstein shows that the problems of antitrust consent decrees have arisen largely from excessively ambitious and "uneconomic" applications of the antitrust laws themselves. When antitrust law concerns itself with subtle and complex forms of business conduct whose anticompetitive effect depends on observation and interpretation—such as "predatory price competition" and the commercial practices of firms with large market shares—the administration of consent decrees tends to encompass a wide range of business-management decisions, presenting many opportunities for mission-creep and counterproductive results. When antitrust is limited to unambiguously anticompetitive conduct, or in any event to highly specific conduct—such as price-fixing and other forms of cartelization and, in the case of unilateral (single-firm) conduct, specific contract restrictions which are to be proscribed or abandoned—consent decrees are crisp and concise and their administration is confined and unproblematic. To which Professor Epstein wisely adds: New market entry is almost always a more effective remedy to the original antitrust complaint than ongoing regulation of the incumbent firms, and time limits on consent decrees may be an effective means to ensuring that the natural competitive process is permitted to run its course.

Professor Epstein's study began as commissioned research for the Microsoft Corporation. When he had completed his manuscript, he shared it with several academic colleagues, including those at the American Enterprise Institute. We immediately saw that he had produced an important original contribution to antitrust scholarship that should be brought to the attention of a wider audience, and were delighted when he agreed to expand on his manuscript for publication. I must register the usual disclaimer that the arguments, conclusions, and recommendations set forth here are independent of, and may or may not coincide with, the views of the Microsoft Corporation. At the same time, I would like to thank the firm's executives for using their own, immediate and practical interest in antitrust consent decrees as the occasion for sponsoring such a capacious and erudite analysis of the subject.

CHRISTOPHER DEMUTH
President
American Enterprise Institute
for Public Policy Research

Acknowledgments

This work was done with the financial support of Microsoft Corporation, which did not review or oversee the conclusions in this study. I should like to thank Michael Greve of the AEI for his exacting editing of the manuscript and Anne Layne-Farrar and Nadia Hussaini of LECG for their unfailing help in the preparation of this manuscript. Kayvan Narouzi, University of Chicago Law School, class of 2009, gave the manuscript one final close read.

Introduction

Judicial consent decrees play a significant role in modern law, especially in the contentious area of antitrust law. By some measures, over 60 percent of antitrust disputes are resolved (more or less, as we shall see) by means of consent decrees.[1] If anything, that raw number understates their economic and institutional significance. Antitrust decrees have governed—and sometimes restructured—entire industries, often over a period of several decades. This study examines several of the most famous sagas, involving industries from meatpacking to shoe machinery to telecommunications to computer operating systems. The direct effects of consent decrees in these sprawling disputes are revealed most directly—though not always in ways that are easily quantified—in the structure of the affected industries, and in the lines of the consumers whom they serve. But their effects are broader still. The mere threat of government antitrust actions may have a large (if hard to measure) impact on the decisions of major corporations—which as "dominant firms" tend to bear the brunt of antitrust litigation generally— to enter new lines of business or to expand their presence in older ones. In my view, the strongest defense for an open economy lies not in legal enforcement, but in free entry and exit of firms in the relevant market. To the extent that consent decrees restrict those practices, they necessarily affect adversely the climate for business investment and innovation.

Much past writing on antitrust and on consent decrees has focused on the recurrent question of what standard of review is proper for modification or termination of a decree. Usually that question is studied in isolation, without any sustained analysis of the factual and legal disputes that gave rise to the decree. I delve in detail into these matters in the conviction that a systematic understanding of why antitrust consent decrees succeed or fail turns on much more than the modification question. I hope to offer an analysis of the role consent decrees play in the antitrust law, with the emphasis more on function and less on doctrine.

While past judicial practices provide much reason for distress, my basic thesis is a cheerful one: We have seen by and large a constructive and welcome change in attitude toward consent decrees, which largely parallels a more restrained attitude about the risks and benefits of antitrust intervention in general. Earlier judges and commentators in the United States placed a great confidence in the ability of the antitrust laws to rectify the ills of American industry. Government lawyers proposed, and judges eagerly embraced, concerted efforts to restructure entire industries to advance the needs of consumers and the public at large. My objection to that way of doing business is not to its implicit standard of social welfare, but rather to the naïve assumption that aggressive antitrust enforcement is the invariant path to that laudable end. Too often, it is not. Antitrust exuberance has frequently led to an expansive view of the remedial role of court cases, which all too often has proved counter-productive. Historically, of course, many consent decrees have come and gone without incident, precisely because they were well-tailored to the situation at hand, and adhered much more closely to the traditional judicial review on the need to avoid complex judicial remedies. These uneventful decisions prove the soundness of the maxim that less is more. All too often, however, antitrust decrees have suffered from an excess of ambition by which too much was attempted, and too little was achieved. Badly framed, sprawling decrees wreaked a great deal of havoc before they were modified or terminated. Especially in high-profile cases, prudence was cast aside in the effort to "get" the antitrust violator. The overall results are tabulated with brief descriptions in the table located in the appendix, History of Antitrust Consent Decrees.

Happily, recent years have brought forth a more guarded estimation of the gains from antitrust intervention. The principal exhibit in support of that cautiously optimistic assessment is the well-known and ongoing litigation involving Microsoft in the federal courts in Washington, D.C. The *Microsoft* cases had two close calls, with two final judgments by district court judges that went far beyond the bounds of reason and good sense. But the steady performance of the Court of Appeals for the District of Columbia and the well-crafted consent decree of Judge Colleen

Kollar-Kotelly have proved a welcome departure from the antitrust imperialism that had too often held sway in this field.

Chapter 1 of this book presents a general analytical framework for how to think about consent decrees in general and antitrust decrees in particular. Chapter 2 examines the history of antitrust decrees. I begin with short treatments of the breakup of Standard Oil, the aluminum industry, and the movie industry. I then consider in more detail (and in rough historical sequence) the prohibition against entry into new lines of business in *Swift & Co. v. United States*; the contractual restrictions and eventual breakup in *United Shoe Machinery*; and the continuous government supervision of the licensing arrangements for musical works. The case studies in chapters 3 and 4 provide a vivid contrast between the two most important antitrust proceedings in modern history: the singularly ill-advised breakup of the Bell System between 1982 and the passage of the Telecommunications Act of 1996, and the far more sensible disposition of the Microsoft litigation. Chapter 5 concludes with the central lessons learned from the more detailed consent decrees study: Less is indeed more.

Why, pray tell, should anyone but historians or antitrust enthusiasts pay attention to the case studies that constitute the bulk of this study—now that the sins of the past have been superseded by more sober-minded antitrust sensibilities? My answer is that no policy advance is irreversible, least of all when potent political factions can be expected to agitate for that reversal. Our culture redounds with constant populist pleas for antitrust attacks on the likes of Wal-Mart on the apparent ground that large and successful firms have built-in insulation against economic risk.[2] Similarly, a number of recent antitrust decisions in the lower courts presage a new era of antitrust activism, which, with a change of administrations, could easily spill over from private to public enforcement.[3] This scenario is not unlikely when, as in the antitrust context, the current synthesis requires a scaling back of public ambitions, a more nuanced understanding of the economic and institutional trade-offs, and a willingness to face down intensely interested constituencies. Policy improvements of this type have a better chance of sticking when they are accompanied by a better understanding of why they, in fact, count as improvements—and why earlier policies, even when advanced with the best of intentions, often produced train wrecks. To understand why less is often more in antitrust, one has to understand that more has often proved less.

1

Theoretical Foundations

The consent decree represents a distinctive and imaginative amalgam: It operates both as a contract between two or more parties to settle disputes between them and as a final judgment of the court that has entered it. It thus marries the flexibility of a private contract to the legal clout of a final judgment. The settlement mechanism spares both sides the risk and expense of a prolonged trial. Incorporating that settlement into a final judgment makes sure that the settlement will hold over time.

The contractual element allows for the same broad scope of substantive provisions that can be found in any private settlement, regardless of subject matter. Ironically, then, the parties have wide latitude in constructing a settlement even where the underlying wrongs take place in a regime, such as antitrust, that is meant to limit freedom of contract, especially among competitors. As with other settlements, consent decrees are governed by the rules of contractual interpretation, and thus must be interpreted in accordance with their "plain meaning" or "explicit language"[1]—except where the language itself breaks down, as it frequently does.

Because of its incorporation into a judgment, a consent decree has a greater level of permanence and authority than an ordinary settlement. First, the enforcement of a private settlement has to run all the risks associated with a civil action for breach of contract. In order to maintain a fresh suit, the injured party has to negotiate the procedural obstacles of jurisdiction, venue, service of process, statute of limitations, discovery, and the like. These difficulties are obviated by a consent decree, which the parties submit in advance to the authority of the court that first approved the decree. Second, a claim for breach of contract is vulnerable to attack on the grounds that the contract does not embody the final agreement, that it has been induced by fraud, and that it does not represent the complete deal between the parties.

Those defenses are unavailing in the context of a consent decree; to attack the validity of the decree is necessarily to impugn the integrity of the court that oversaw the entire process. Third, the remedies for violating a consent decree are more potent than for an ordinary breach of contract. Breach an agreement, and the usual remedies are damages, injunction, and specific performance—if you can get them. Breach a consent decree, and you face, in addition to the ordinary remedies, a contempt of court citation from an irate judge who is invested in the outcome of the case.

The advantages, however, come at a price: Typically, the parties can obtain a consent decree only after their settlement has received some judicial review, which is the functional substitute for the adversarial trial that normally leads up to a final judgment in a contested case. Antitrust consent decrees to which the United States is a party have been governed since 1974 by the Tunney Act. That statute, commonly understood to have codified then existing judicial practice, instructs judges to conduct a "public interest determination" prior to entry of a decree.[2] The act creates a real tension. While a district court judge who is completely passive has failed to discharge his responsibilities under the Tunney Act, a judge who takes over the case displaces (typically) the prosecutor, which in turn may raise serious separation of powers issues. (As the case studies will show, the problem is anything but idle speculation.) No consent decree, however, is freely or casually awarded for the asking. The parties must submit a detailed plan for judicial review, which at a minimum requires some assessment of the impact of the decree not only on the parties to the dispute but also on third parties. In light of that stringent review, consent decrees operate as a close substitute for final judgments, from which they should not be distinguished analytically in any material way. In Justice Benjamin Cardozo's famous words, "The result is all one whether the decree has been entered after litigation or by consent."[3]

Consent Decrees

The hybrid form of the consent decree—part contract, part judicial order—does, however, entail a subtle change in the judiciary's role in designing remedies. An award of damages or specific performance to a victorious plaintiff for some past violation terminates the relationship, and allows the parties to go their separate ways. (For this reason, private antitrust actions never involve consent decrees; the plaintiffs take their treble-damage awards and run.) Consent decrees reflect a much higher level of ambition for the judicial process, illustrated most vividly when they target public institutions that are perceived to have profoundly failed in carrying out their missions. Whether the topic is the racial integration of schools, the oversight of mental hospitals, welfare programs, or prisons, the "one-and-done" response will not work. The objective is a fundamental redirection of public institutions, with an eye toward the elimination of the substandard practices or dangerous conditions that sparked the initial intervention. This ambition necessarily creates enormous stress on the remedial phase of any action, regardless of the underlying nature of the public wrong. The ensuing difficulties can be summarized under the headings of duration, ambition, and complexity.

Duration. Consent decrees often last for too long a period. That compounds difficulties in complex consent decrees that are unsound from their inception. But the passage of time also tends to devalue consent decrees that may have been well-adapted to the original violations. In antitrust, this error is not random in its direction. Technological innovation breaks down monopoly and rarely (if ever) strengthens it. In some cases, the breakdown comes through the convergence of technologies, as when phone, Internet, fax, and cable converge into information neatly encoded in a set of 0's and 1's. In other cases, geographical barriers are reduced as the cost of transportation and communication drops, enlarging the scope of local markets and making it unwise to rely on a static model that computes market share, and hence dominant position, on the basis of current market participation. The erosion of private monopoly power suggests that consent decrees depreciate over time. Any defect in their formulation, however, is not easily corrected by allowing, subject to court approval, their modification in light of changed circumstances. The process is so balky that even relatively lax standards of review do not supply sufficient flexibility.

Ambition. Consent decrees often cut too wide a path, without anchoring their prohibitions to the specific antitrust violations that required the settlement. Their broad reach necessarily invites claims for constant revision and reinterpretation. The process acts as tax on innovation as the parties to the consent decree, and those affected by it, constantly maneuver to escape restrictions that should not have been imposed at all. The moral is that consent decrees should remedy antitrust violations first and foremost. They should not seek to introduce industrial policy through the side door.

Complexity. Often, consent decrees attempt to fine-tune a complex process in ways that add administrative cost and business uncertainty. This long-term rigidity takes its toll on the very competitive processes that the antitrust law is intended to enhance. Every restriction is a barrier to competition, which is more potent when it is backed by government power that cannot be eroded by changes in cost or technology. When consent decrees compel firms to comply with external dictates on how to go about their business, the firms become less effective competitors (assuming they survive the oversight process). Often they are precluded from entering new markets, so that the consent decree operates to insulate established firms from competition. Sometimes they are weighed down with heavy oversight provisions so they cannot adapt to new circumstances within the line of business that remains open to them.

The common response, among both courts and legal scholars, has been to take the form of the consent decree for granted, while tinkering with the standards for the judicial modification of such decrees. In its initial foray into consent decrees in *United States v. Swift & Co.* (1932), an important antitrust case that I will examine in chapter 2, the Supreme Court laid down as its general rule that "nothing less than a clear showing of grievous wrong evoked by new and unforeseen conditions" is sufficient to justify either modifying or terminating a consent decree.[4] Six decades later, in *Rufo v. Inmates of Suffolk County Jail* (1992), the Supreme Court self-consciously held that the large public stake in these institutions justified a more flexible approach to help ensure that public institutions operate in accordance with appropriate standards of safety and efficiency.[5] The issue left hanging in *Rufo* was whether the strict *Swift & Co.* standard survived in the antitrust and commercial area now that it had been effectively shunted aside in institutional cases.[6] The lower courts have uniformly answered that question in the negative, largely on the grounds that the language for the modification of equitable decrees in the Federal Rules of Civil Procedure does not vary by subject matter.[7] Functionally, the courts have argued that flexible decrees are better able to take into account changed circumstances than the more restrictive *Swift* standard.

My sense is that in dealing with antitrust consent decrees (or the formal, final judgments for which they are a substitute), there is relatively low payoff in looking at how courts have handled cases that involve the redress of constitutional violations by public entities. The general problems of duration, ambition, and complexity have routinely occurred in both settings. Below the conceptual stratosphere, however, the differences dominate. Institutional cases arise over the concerns of discrete and insular minorities, who are often without political power. These individuals and groups are pitted against government agencies that operate under political and budgetary pressures that could easily lead them to stray from their legal duties. The plaintiffs' claims, meanwhile, bump up against legitimate claims of democratic governance: If judicial decrees govern public institutions for years and perhaps decades, why hold elections?[8]

None of these factors is in play in antitrust decrees. The specter of a breakdown in public administration does not wait in the wings, and the usual plaintiff is the United States government. It seems best to take these differences into account in drafting antitrust consent decrees. Armed with the knowledge from past experiences, the parties could stipulate for the appropriate degree of flexibility in each case. The learned disquisitions on the appropriate attitude toward consent decrees could be treated simply as default terms that should be displaced when the initial decree (like any other contract) introduces provisions intended to deal with future uncertainty. Historically, however, it has not been common for consent decrees to build in their own standards for modification. And, mysteriously, there is little pause in the decided cases to ask whether that decision is a good or a bad thing. The tacit assumption seems to be that structural remedies should be permanent—even when market forces are not.

In that context and setting, the flexible *Rufo* standard should not necessarily be rejected.[9] But I confess that, at the end of the day, I have no strong stake in the ongoing doctrinal fight over the proper standard of judicial review and decree modification. Rather, my central point is that the sound administration of consent decrees depends in all events on an appreciation of the connection between the underlying substantive violation and the proposed remedial solution.

The history of antitrust consent decrees demonstrates, first, the importance of keeping a simple remedial structure. The appropriate guidelines are the traditional remedial rules that have long been applied both at common law and in courts of equity. The key to success is to guard against the dangers of continuous judicial supervision in exchange for a set of remedies that wrap up these disputes as soon as possible after a consent decree has been entered. The greater the level of ambition, the more serious the shipwrecks that follow.

The history of consent decrees demonstrates, second, the need to have some realistic sense of the strengths and weaknesses of antitrust law. Consent decrees represent not just bargaining in the shadow of the law, but bargaining in the presence of the law. In antitrust contexts, it is usually a safe bet that professional and experienced counsel on both sides of the case have mastered the legal and factual issues in question, reducing the chance of slippage between the rights that the law gives to each party, and the pound of flesh that each exacts in settlement.[10] This entails that consent decrees will reflect not only the strength of the antitrust laws, but also inherit their weaknesses. Where the underlying decision is sound, the consent decree can add to its success. But any legal mistakes in terms of substantive principles or remedial choices are magnified by the very effectiveness of the consent decree.

Remedies

The Supreme Court has phrased the canonical questions on the choice of remedy for antitrust violations as follows: "to unfetter a market from anticompetitive conduct,"[11] "to terminate the illegal monopoly, deny the defendant the fruits of its statutory violation, and ensure that there remain no practices likely to result in monopolization of the future."[12] These statements describe—and limit—the objectives of antitrust enforcement, but give little guidance as to the proper means toward those ends. Unfortunately, they have been aggressively read to say that any restriction on firm practices that moves in this direction should be vigorously pursued, regardless of its collateral consequences. I urge a different reading. Antitrust remedies, in the context of consent decrees or elsewhere, should be closely tailored to the underlying violations. That choice of remedies should, more-over, be guided by the same considerations of judicial economy that have guided the law of remedies in general, so that the risks and errors of exces-sive intrusion should be weighted equally with those of underinclusion.

Historically, the development of legal remedies was tied up with the division of power between the common-law courts and the courts of equity. The common-law courts had jurisdiction over disputes that involved what a defendant took or destroyed, or breach of contract. The available reme-dies were, in general, tailored narrowly to the underlying wrong. If some-one took your property, the legal remedy required him to give it back. If he damaged but did not destroy the property, a plaintiff would recover the property with allowance for the damage, or else recover the full price of the property, the title to which then went over to the defendant. These remedies were designed to minimize the inquiries that courts had to make into the underlying facts of the case. Once the remedy had been imposed, moreover, little or no subsequent judicial involvement was nec-essary. The owner who was restored to his property could proceed as though it had never been taken. The wrongdoer who had restored the property could resume his normal life. This simple conception of corrective justice had as its goal the restoration of the status quo ante whenever that was possible.

In cases that involve personal injury or property destruction, restora-tion is no longer available, so some form of cash compensation is required. Usually, this requires some estimation of property loss, which can become complex when the property has some distinctive use or subjective value to its owner. The damage calculations for personal injuries are more compli-cated still. And in cases of death or permanent injury, there is no way to make good on the general formula that requires the defendant to restore the plaintiff to the same level of well-being that he had before the accident. So a cottage industry is born that seeks to estimate what these damages would be, taking into account the inherent uncertainty in the extent or duration of pain, the length of life, the level of future medical bills and other expenses, and the future loss of earnings. The estimation of these figures is part art, part science.[13] Still, the common-law rules did as much as they could to make all damage calculations a one-shot affair that allowed parties to go their separate ways at the conclusion of a lawsuit. The standard remedy was and is lump-sum damages. The parties may themselves opt for structured or annuity settlements, but only against a background of a legal system that requires lump-sum payments to discharge all obligations. All outstanding issues are resolved at once.

Contract damage actions take the same form. There is much disagreement on whether the background rule of damages requires that the party in breach pay that sum of money sufficient to put the plaintiff in the same position he enjoyed before the contract was entered into—so-called reliance damages—or whether the right standard requires the defendant to pay the plaintiff a sum of money sufficient to put the plaintiff in the position he would have enjoyed if the contract had been performed.[14] Both standards, however, call for a lump-sum payment that allows the parties to go their separate ways after the dispute is resolved, free of judicial supervision. In many (though not enough) cases the parties are allowed to stipulate damages by some formula, which is almost always structured so as to call for lump-sum payments that obviate the need to figure out whether, and if so how, the injured party should have mitigated the loss in question. For example, the typical termination agreement in the employment context calls for so much severance pay for each year of employment, after which the parties have no further connections. In short, lump-sum payments dominate this area as well.

We still have to account for the other side of the traditional legal system, the courts of equity. These originally developed when the English chancellor—a high official lawyer to the Crown—was asked for special remedies when the common-law provision of damages was thought to be inadequate. The traditional legal formulation said that equitable remedies acted "on the person" of the defendant and required him to do or refrain from certain acts. The two major forms of relief were the injunction, which stops a defendant from doing a particular act; and specific performance, which requires a party to perform a particular act.[15] The use of these remedies exhibited the same effort for swift dispute resolution that characterized the common-law remedies of restitution and damages.

Specific performance represents the ideal that a party who reneges on a promise should, to the extent that the law is able, be forced to perform that promise and not treat common-law damages as an option to buy his way out of a binding commitment. The remedy was commonly used in land-sale contracts, where the point was to transfer the title to land from the seller to the buyer, typically at the instance of either.[16] One advantage of specific performance is that it avoided the knotty questions of figuring out just what level of damages should be provided to a seller who finds it difficult to buy a new house or factory, or to a buyer who cannot relocate because the seller has decided not to convey the property sold. But note again the dominant pattern: Transfer of title, followed by recordation, is a clean deal which requires no oversight by the court once the transaction is complete. Damages can then be awarded to pick up the slack, given that specific performance does not compensate for the inconvenience and additional costs that invariably follow from delay. The level of judicial resources spent in supervising an ongoing transaction is at a minimum, and parties who bargain in the shadow of the law will make the conveyance without resort to judicial compulsion.

The situation takes on a different coloration when the question is whether a court should order specific enforcement of a partnership agreement or an employment contract.[17] The usual answer was sharply in the negative. Partnerships (and to a lesser extent employment contracts) are continuing, open-ended relationships whose success depends on the parties' mutual trust. Specific enforcement is ill-suited to this situation because no amount of judicial oversight can make up for the loss of trust between parties. But it hardly follows that damages should be the only remedy, especially if the breach of an employment contract is followed by an employee's decision to go into competition with his former employer, either as an independent firm or as an employee of a rival. In these cases, the equitable injunction stops the migration to the rival firm and thus limits the collateral damage caused by the contractual breach.[18] In its clean form, the injunction requires no continuous judicial supervision of the activities of the enjoined party, who now has an additional inducement to patch up relationships with a former employer (especially since damages are still available for the breach). These rules make more sense, in my view, than the efforts of the modern labor and antidiscrimination laws, which treat reinstatement as a standard remedy—one that can require intense judicial oversight in circumstances where the level of trust between the parties is low.

The basic analysis carries over to other forms of remedy. The law of mortgages involves intervention in the relationship between a borrower and a creditor. But the remedies are similar to specific performance in property transactions. Foreclosure involves the surrender of all interest in the mortgaged property to the lender, but does not involve a continuous relationship between the parties. The reciprocal remedy of redemption allows the borrower to remove the lien on the property once the loan has been paid off. Like foreclosure, it makes a clean separation between the parties. The law of nuisance, for another example, addresses not only the occasional instance of fumes or pollution that crosses boundaries, but also the continuing threat of this wrong, which is expensive to remedy with multiple, periodic actions in damages. Injunctive relief, which requires the conduct to stop, does not contemplate a continuing relationship between the parties but a continuing separation, which is easy to monitor and enforce. Often, injunctions are not fully categorical. More noise may be allowed during the day than at night, for instance.[19] But these conditions and variations do not deviate from the golden rule that confines the remedies to those behaviors that can be easily observed and stopped by a court.

The pattern is unmistakable: The entire traditional system of remedies is geared to maximize the freedom of the parties after the imposition of the remedy, and to minimize the judicial resources needed to keep those parties apart. The success of the system lies in its high level of reliability, coupled with its low level of ambition. In principle, this remedial frame of mind can be carried over to consent decrees, which are in their inception equitable remedies as applied to antitrust cases. Antitrust decrees are in some sense unique because of their impact on third parties and the public interest. Yet a moment's reflection shows that the equitable remedies of specific performance and injunction also have to take account of third-party interests. The remedy in an employment dispute will often prevent one worker from going to work for a competitor, which raises questions close to those of the antitrust laws. (Indeed, one reason to be reluctant to enforce anticompete clauses is that they stifle competition, just as one reason to enforce them is that they will induce the initial employer to make greater investments in the employees whose mobility is so limited.) Similarly, injunctions against nuisances will influence the behavior of the enjoined firm's competitors and of other parties that derive indirect benefit from the enforcement of an injunction. Stated simply, any sensible and potent remedy will have third-party effects. That does not undermine the strong case for legal remedies that produce clean breaks and easy judicial oversight, in antitrust as elsewhere.

Antitrust

General considerations of legal philosophy will tend to influence one's view of consent decrees. My classical liberal orientation leaves me uneasy about *any* use of the antitrust laws.[20] The fundamental obligation of society is to minimize the use of force or fraud. The antitrust laws do not typically address these issues at all, and when they do, they duplicate the traditional remedies for misrepresentation, patent infringement, defamation, and the like. The challenge is to identify the cases in which the use of the antitrust laws promises an overall improvement from this simpler and cheaper legal regime. Meeting that challenge requires breaking down the general antitrust laws into two parts, roughly corresponding to section 1 and section 2 of the Sherman Act.[21]

Section 1 is designed to address various forms of horizontal arrangements that result in a restriction of output, an increase in price, a division of territories, and a reduction in overall social welfare. Even within this domain of horizontal restraints, it is far from clear that antitrust law has a strong and positive social role to play. Legal remedies are always costly, and there are false positives and negatives in sorting through the complex evidence to see whether or not the parties have entered into some subterranean agreement to divide territories or to rig prices. It is easy to find cases where courts have ignored overwhelming evidence of collusive behavior, and others in which they are prepared to infer collusion—or allow a case to proceed so that a jury may infer collusion—on laughably weak evidence.[22] Unfortunately, the errors in both directions do not cancel each other out—they cumulate. The ultimate question for legal enforcement, therefore, is not simply whether cartels are inimical to social welfare. It is whether the gains from using criminal sanctions or private treble-damage actions are worth the candle in light of the high error and administrative costs.[23]

Putting aside those global doubts about the efficacy of antitrust law, however, consent decrees that guard against cartels and other forms of collusive behavior set the gold standard of antitrust enforcement. First, a solid economic theory explains why a prohibition against various forms of collusive conduct is conducive to overall social welfare. Second, and strikingly, the legal responses to these arrangements fit neatly into the cautious remedial strategy set out above. The first form of relief is damages (whether or not trebled is for this point not relevant) for the past harm that the cartel has worked. The second form is injunctive relief, which simply prohibits future cooperation among cartel members. Both forms of relief meet the standards for sensible remedies. The only difficulty with damages is their calculation, which is inescapable under any legal system. Antitrust injunctions do not require any explicit form of judicial oversight, and are indeed typically easier to enforce than injunctions against nuisances that might vary with particular circumstances. Finally, the duration of the remedy poses no particular risks. No matter what the changes in technology and market structure, there is little reason to think that prohibitions against future cartelization will be rendered obsolete with the passage of time. These remedies thus reach low-hanging fruit. A simple remedial structure is sufficient to counteract the major antitrust risk. Many decrees have taken this form. They have usually presented few enforcement difficulties and, to my knowledge, have not raised any requests for judicial modification.

The major problems with consent decrees arise in the section 2 context— that is, in connection with more adventurous antitrust theories and with the substantive provisions that prohibit certain unilateral practices of dominant firms. With unilateral practices, no strong economic theory—of the sort that condemns price-fixing and often cartel arrangements among competitors— is available.[24] And, as it turns out, the antitrust doctrines that are troublesome on the substantive side are also troublesome on the remedial side.

High on this list are predation, exclusive dealing, and tie-in arrangements. In these cases, the key problems of enforcement usually do not involve questions of evidence. It is difficult for a single firm (or for a group working in combination) to conceal the low prices it wishes to offer consumers to drive rivals out of the market. Likewise, exclusive-dealing and tie-in arrangements are routinely evident on the face of the transaction. The hard question in all these cases is to show that the practices are harmful to social welfare in the first place.

The prohibition against predation, for example, is said to cover cases where a dominant firm sells goods at below marginal cost in order to obtain a monopoly down the road by driving out all competitors today.[25] It is hard to see, though, how firms that lose huge amounts today will be able to recoup their losses down the road—when they have no way to prevent other entrants from jumping back into the market once they raise their prices above competitive levels.[26] These substantive difficulties make it hard to see how one could fashion an intelligent consent decree. By definition, predation will work only if it drives out rivals in the short run, and barriers exist to prevent their return in the long run. Just how long, then, should a consent decree last? More importantly, it is unclear how to frame its substantive provisions. Barring a firm from pricing below marginal cost requires constant supervision over matters that are easier to state than to calculate or observe. It is quite likely that any such decree could cut against a firm's ability to reduce prices *toward* marginal cost in ways that operate to long-term social advantage. In short, the remedial difficulties complicate the case for an already dubious substantive theory.

Similar observations apply to tie-in and exclusive-dealing arrangements. There is nothing unsound about imposing some restraints on pricing or terms (as appropriate) for a firm whose dominant position gives it effective control over a market. The law of common carriers, which requires them to take customers on reasonable and nondiscriminatory terms, is an age-old legal principle, albeit one that operates less through the antitrust laws and more through traditional systems of rate regulation.[27] Still, section 2 cases over unilateral restraints on trade give rise to a trade-off between restraint and efficiency that is not present in the easy section 1 cases.[28] Inevitably, they impose on dominant firms restrictions on market practices that are routinely adopted by other firms within the industry. Presumably, those practices have at least some efficiency properties. Yet the law imposes stiff treble-damage penalties, even though the social harm is far less than that of ordinary cartels—if, indeed, there is any harm at all. Unlike many cartel arrangements, moreover, prices and contractual arrangements are never secret, so the trebling of damages can no longer be justified as an effort to offset the costs of detection.

The true remedial difficulty, however, is not with lump-sum damages, which operate in this context the same way that they do in any other. The problem lies in the type of injunctive relief that is granted as part of a final judgment or consent degree. Instead of simply telling the parties that they are no longer allowed to collude, a court now either chooses to, or is compelled to, craft some more adventurous antitrust remedy that starts to abut against the difficulties that led courts of equity to rein in their ambition in employment and partnership contexts. The specific prohibitions are more complex in form, and hence more difficult to police. In addition, their expected durability will have to shrink, as shifts in technology and market conditions could easily undercut the wisdom of the initial arrangements. Accordingly, there will be greater pressure on the courts to modify the initial decree and to relax its restrictions. Yet there is no easy judicial standard to determine when such modifications should be allowed, particularly over objections from parties who might be adversely affected by the change in market structure. Put simply, the benefits of these adventurous decrees are far lower than those of a simple injunction against cartel behavior, while the costs of running the system increase sharply. There comes a point at which the lines cross. The case studies that follow illustrate many of the pitfalls that beset the use of antitrust decrees.

2

Case Studies

Robert Crandall and Clifford Winston have compiled short and convenient summaries of three famous cases, which from an economic perspective by and large reinforce the basic conclusion set out above.[1] The slow and ponderous pace of antitrust litigation is such that the passage of time and the transformation of technology render consent decrees either inconsequential or counterproductive. The decidedly mixed results of aggressive antitrust enforcement are further illustrated by the protracted struggles that marked four important consent decree cases that I will examine in greater detail: *Swift & Co.*, which dealt with the regulation and breakup of the great meatpacking companies; the *United Shoe Machinery* case, in which the United States pursued United Shoe Machinery for over fifty years before it achieved the breakup of an efficient competitor in an ever more global world market; the ASCAP/BMI saga, where the United States was never able to create efficient parity between the two rival organizations that were formed to secure the effective distribution of music to the broadcast industry; and the breakup of the old AT&T network under Judge Harold Greene's famous consent decree.

Some Thumbnail Accounts

Standard Oil. In the great *Standard Oil* case,[2] the government sought relief against Rockefeller's Standard Oil Company for predatory practices against its competitors and for hardnosed dealings with pipelines and transportation facilities, where its intention was to foreclose the use of these essential facilities by rivals. Once the firm had been found guilty of monopolization, the discussion turned to remedy. Instead of targeting relief against the

18

specific practices, the remedy chosen called for Standard Oil's breakup into thirty-eight separate companies, which were supposed to be independent of each other but which were, in fact, subject to some common retained control by the Rockefeller interests.

It is worth noting that the claims of predation had been largely discredited, for it was easier for Standard Oil to buy out its rivals with cash payments than to try to run them out of business with low prices.[3] Moreover, since neither oil production nor refining is a network industry, no market share is large enough to preclude new entry by a rival with more efficient production techniques. The price umbrella that any monopoly throws over competitors is itself a powerful spur to new entry that, unlike the situation in network industries, in no way depends on the cooperation of others. It is therefore noteworthy, but not surprising, that Standard Oil's market share dropped from 64 percent to 50 percent between 1911 and 1920, after the decree was put into place. But by the same token it had previously fallen from 82 percent to 64 percent between 1899 and 1911. The steady downward trend suggests that the consent decree had little effect.

Crandall and Winston seem correct in concluding that while a breakup might have been of value twelve years earlier, it was at most "benign" when it came. But "too little, too late" does not in this context reflect a mistake in judgment by government officials. It reflects the glacial pace of antitrust litigation in general.

Alcoa. Another famous consent decree case involved the breakup of the Aluminum Company of America (Alcoa), which had been formed in the early 1900s through a combination of American and Canadian interests. Alcoa had obtained extensive control over industry processes from the mining of bauxite (aluminum ore) to the fabrication of aluminum ingot into specific products such as sheet, tube, and wire. In 1912 Alcoa signed a consent decree that had both horizontal and vertical aspects. On the horizontal side, Alcoa agreed to divest itself of its Canadian subsidiary and to refrain from mergers or other collusive agreements, leaving it the possibility of expansion only through internal growth. On the vertical side, Alcoa agreed to stipulations that affected both its upstream and downstream operations. Upstream, it terminated long-term supply contracts with the chemical companies from which it had acquired bauxite. Downstream, it agreed not to withhold its ingot from any company that fabricated end-products in competition with the firm. As Crandall and Winston point out, the market for aluminum was, given the economies of scale in mining operations, too small to support more than a single major supplier, so that by 1937 Alcoa's share of the ingot market still remained at a hefty 90 percent of overall production.

Frustrated by the slow pace of change, the United States filed a new suit charging Alcoa with illegal monopolization under section 2 of the Sherman Act. That charge was sustained in a famous Learned Hand decision in *United States v. Aluminum Company of America.*[4] The remedy was postponed until the conclusion of the Second World War, when the shape of the market was effectively changed once the United States sold to Reynolds Metals and Kaiser Aluminum the plants that it had constructed in the interim for all phases of aluminum reduction, smelting, and fabrication. By this time, however, the demand for aluminum products had grown, so that economies of scale in production no longer precluded the entry of additional firms with or without government assistance.

Once again, the shifts in the landscape had more to do with the transformation of the aluminum industry than with the consent decree. Indeed, after three more companies entered the aluminum market in the early 1950s, the district court in 1956 declined to renew the decree for another five-year term. Alcoa's market share had dropped by over 50 percent of what it was in 1937, even though its output increased fourfold. Clearly, the economies of scale mattered a great deal. In an important sense, then, the case looks very much like a replay of *Standard Oil.* It is unlikely that any firm that lacks the power to block entry will be able to maintain its monopoly position in the long run.

Paramount Pictures. The same uncertain outcome characterizes the ambitious government action that resulted in the breakup of the movie industry in the wake of the U.S. Supreme Court's 1948 decision in *United States v. Paramount Pictures Inc.* This complex case against the major motion picture studios—Columbia, Paramount, Loews, Universal, and United Artists— challenged a wealth of practices, including "joint ownership of theaters by distributors and exhibitors, theater pooling agreements, formula deals, master agreements and franchises, block booking, and discrimination between exhibitors in the terms of master agreements."[5] Central to the dispute was the studios' participation in horizontal and vertical restraints of trade with respect to the licensing of their copyrighted films to distributors, and through them to exhibitors.

One point of little doubt was that the copyright monopoly allowed each copyright holder, acting separately, to exploit whatever economic strength it had with respect to its own intellectual property, but not to engage in a combination that covered multiple works—a bedrock proposition that lies at the intersection of intellectual property and antitrust laws.[6] That argument doomed the horizontal fixing of prices at the studio level. Vertically, each studio through its distribution arm set minimum prices that the motion-picture exhibitors could charge their customers, regardless of whether the license was based on a fixed fee or a percentage of sales. Combined, the two practices gave the vertical arrangement the appearance of sustaining a horizontal monopoly at the exhibitor level, a result that would be more difficult to defend if there had been no coordination in pricing at the producer level.

In light of the evident antitrust violations, the key question was the remedy. The simple approach here called for an injunction against price-fixing agreements among the distributors and, more controversially, the restriction of downstream control by the producers. The Supreme Court, speaking through Justice William O. Douglas, did not stop there, but concluded that the purpose of antitrust law "does not end with enjoining continuance of the unlawful restraints nor with dissolving the combination which launched the conspiracy. Its function includes undoing what the conspiracy achieved."[7] Once the case was remanded, each of the producers divested itself of all its theaters—but for whose benefit? The radical restructuring of the industry did not result in lower movie prices, nor did it reduce concentration at the producer level. The revised consent agreements increased the percentage of the take held by the distributors, but that number was in and of itself of little significance; when the distributors were owned by the studios, the allocation of profits reflected internal accounting as much as or more than, economic reality. It is hard to find any systematic gain from the divesture, even if the price-fixing charges were fully vindicated.

The Meatpacking Industry: *United States v. Swift & Co.*

United States v. Swift (1932) is most frequently cited for the tough attitude it takes toward contract modification, but it is at least as important for what it tells us about the proper approach to consent decrees. It arose out of a federal antitrust action filed in February 1920 against Swift and four other leading meatpackers in the United States to dissolve the cooperative arrangements that had grown up among them. The companies' activities had been under constant public scrutiny since the turn of the century, and previous suits had been brought against Swift, Armour, and other meatpackers in an effort to curb their monopolistic practices.[8] The Wilson administration continued to put pressure on the industry during the First World War and, in 1917, asked the Federal Trade Commission to investigate the meatpackers' business practices. In 1919, the FTC report concluded that the major firms had a monopolistic control over the American meat industry and, moreover, had the intent and the means of monopolizing other product markets. The report became the template for the Wilson administration's 1920 antitrust complaint. The government alleged that the firms had conspired to suppress competition in the market for both livestock and meat products and were intent upon extending their conspiracy into other areas, including "fish, vegetables, either fresh or canned, fruits, cereals, milk, poultry, butter, eggs, cheese and other substitute foods ordinarily handled by wholesale grocers or produce dealers," in part through "their ownership of refrigerator cars and branch houses, as well as other facilities."[9]

In addition, the initial government suit made implicit reference to a theory of predation, which noted that whenever the defendant companies lacked sufficient control over the collateral facilities on which their rivals outside the meat industry depended, they "had recourse to the expedient of fixing prices so low over temporary periods of time as to eliminate competition by rivals less favorably situated."[10] We thus have a broad attack that combined three different theories of varying degrees of strength: the cartel, the claim of vertical integration, and the claim of predation, in descending order of antitrust salience.

By prearrangement, a consent decree was entered the day the complaint was filed. It contained an unexceptionable prohibition against further collusion among the parties, but went on to enjoin the defending companies

> both *severally* and jointly from (1) holding any interest in pub-
> lic stockyard companies, stockyard terminal railroads, or market
> newspapers, (2) engaging in, or holding any interest in, the
> business of manufacturing, selling or transporting any of 114
> enumerated food products, (principally fish, vegetables, fruit,
> and groceries), and thirty other articles unrelated to the meat
> packing industry, (3) using or permitting others to use their dis-
> tributive facilities for the handling of any of these enumerated
> articles, (4) selling meat at retail, (5) holding any interest in any
> public cold storage plant, and (6) selling fresh milk or cream.[11]

It was understood at the time that had the case gone to trial, these additional stipulations could not have been imposed, because none of the activities were regarded as illegal under the antitrust laws.[12] The firms' power in
the collateral markets was far less than in the meat industry, and any effort
to succeed would have encountered stiff competition from a broad range of
other firms, many of them sophisticated and well-capitalized.

How should one think about the soundness of this decree? At the
outset, different economic considerations apply to joint conduct and sole
conduct. The *Swift* decree, however, which was directed initially toward the
combined action of the defendants, is explicitly structured so as to prevent
each of the companies from engaging in many different forms of conduct on
an individual basis. The obvious question is why there is any social risk
from unilateral conduct of the sort that is undertaken here.

Peter C. Carstenson has contended that the decree had little adverse
effect on the growth and development of either the grocery or the meat
industry. As part of his general effort to discredit the thesis that aggressive
antitrust enforcement has had adverse effects on the American economy,
Carstenson argues that the impact of the decree

> seems to have been minimal. In a broader perspective, it seems
> unlikely that it had any significant negative effect. Other inno-
> vators emerged to develop supermarkets and to produce broad

lines of grocery products that achieved the efficiencies the pack-
ers sought through merger. There is no evidence that the decree
caused inefficiency in any line of business. If anything, one can
argue that by limiting the power of the largest enterprises in the
food business, the decree may have created, at the margin, a less
risky context for other, smaller firms to innovate and develop.
The decree, therefore, maximized interproduct competition.[13]

In one sense this position has to be correct. A consent decree only binds
the parties, and, unlike legislative restrictions on entry, does not protect
incumbents from anyone else. But to say that the decree did not have disas-
trous consequences does not establish that it introduced any important or
enduring structural reform. The mistake is this: If Swift had never entered
into any combination with its fellow meatpackers, it could have decided on
an individual basis to enter into all the product markets, including the wholesale and retail grocery business, from which the decree excluded it. The same
is true of the other members of the cartel, especially Armour & Co. Each of
the firms is allowed to compete separately in the meat businesses in which
they held separately large market shares. Yet none are allowed to enter any
new markets in which they have a negligible market share.

It is easy to see what is going on here by looking at the caption of the
second suit consolidated with the claim of the United States: *National
Wholesale Grocers Association v. Swift & Co.*, naming one of the two "associations of wholesale grocers, which intervened to oppose the application."[14]
These organizations had obvious anticompetitive motives to keep the meat
companies off their turf. As in many other cases, the structure of the decree,
by treating individual and concerted conduct in the same fashion, worked
as an effective barrier to entry of firms with built-in cost advantages.
Whatever the supposed risks of concerted conduct in dealing with vertical
restraints, exclusive dealing, or predation, these do not carry over to actions
of individual firms, none of whom occupied anything close to a dominant
position in the markets from which the decree bars them. The decree is a
vivid example of how antitrust prosecutions and consent decrees can be
hijacked for anticompetitive purposes.

Swift has a second dimension: How do the restrictions hold up over
time? There is no problem on that score with respect to the anticollusion

provisions. But the situation is quite different with respect to restraints on individual entry into new markets. It is quite easy to envision situations in which the entry right is forfeited in fevered settlement negotiations with the United States so as to escape serious financial penalties for collusive behavior. Thus, the *Swift* decree contained the usual, but critical, boilerplate provisions that the decree "shall not constitute or be considered as an adjudication that the defendants, or any of them, have in fact violated any law of the United States."[15]

But the value of the entry right to the bound firm, and the social gain that comes from that new entry, is not constant over time and circumstances. The *Swift* decree made it impossible for Armour & Co. to perform contracts under which it had agreed to buy canned fruit from the California Co-Operative Canneries, which occupied a different market niche from the wholesale grocers. As their interests were aligned with Armour, the canneries sought to vacate the decree on a series of technical objections on jurisdiction and intervention, which the Supreme Court rejected in two unanimous decisions written by Justice Louis D. Brandeis that denied that the original consent decree was void from its inception.[16] During the 1920s, there was some thought of relaxing the restriction against doing business in groceries, but the idea was not adopted in part because of the opposition of Herbert Hoover in his capacity as "food administrator."[17]

Eventually, the original defendants attempted to modify the original decree and to lift the restraints on their ability to enter the prohibited lines of business. They requested that the companies

> be permitted (1) to own and operate retail meat markets; (2) to own stock in stockyard companies and terminal railroads; (3) to manufacture, sell and deal in the 144 articles specified in paragraph fourth of the decree, which for convenience will be spoken of as "groceries;" (4) to use or permit others to use their distributive facilities in handling such commodities.[18]

The district court refused to remove the restrictions in clauses (1) and (2), which related to the effort of each company to expand its presence in the meat markets. Here there is at least some specter of vertical integration (though no clear explanation as to why individual entry by firms without dominant market position should count as a restrictive practice, given the cost savings that such integration can achieve). But the trial court did relax the restrictions contained in requests (3) and (4), which prevented the expansion of Swift and Armour into unrelated businesses where they had no market power at all.

The Supreme Court (with three justices recused, including Chief Justice Charles E. Hughes, who had argued the case for Swift earlier) reversed the decision below by a four to two vote, insofar as it released the firms from their obligations. In principle, the Court said, a court of equity had "inherent" jurisdiction to modify decrees to take into account changed circumstances, even if that power was not specifically reserved in the original judgment. But the exercise of that power, the Court continued, must depend on a clear showing that those changed circumstances do exist.

Justice Cardozo took the view that the changed circumstances in this case did not affect the binding force of the decree. In his view, the Justice Department's insistence that the original decree apply to both concerted and individual action was not a minor or evanescent portion of the decree. Rather,

> to curb the aggressions of the huge units that would remain, there was to be a check upon their power, even though acting independently, to wage a war of extermination against dealers weaker than themselves. We do not turn aside to inquire whether some of these restraints upon separate as distinguished from joint action could have been opposed with success if the defendants had offered opposition. Instead, they chose to consent, and the injunction, right or wrong, became the judgment of the court.[19]

In effect, the standard of review for setting aside a consent decree is higher than that needed to enter it in the first place, given the common (and generally sensible) adherence to the principle of res judicata. But it is important to set the value of finality in a broader context. That value should be extraordinarily high against a challenge to an initial determination of liability or to damages for completed transactions. Liability depends only on past acts; changed conditions cannot fortify or undermine the earlier decision. But that is not the case with injunctions against future conduct that runs for an indefinite period of time. One might as well say that the decision of a zoning board not to allow a new development on a given site in 1920 should be binding in 1932 when the overall area has been subject to new development. Res judicata has always been applied with a good deal more caution where the facts shift over time.

In applying this principle, it seems clear that one could not seek to set aside the initial decree ten years later on the grounds that its basic premise was flawed. Perhaps there was no way that Swift or Armour could have strong-armed the competition by acting separately when each would have to make good against the competition that the other had offered. But that was true in 1920 and would not change later on, unless, of course, one or the other had gone out of business. The changed circumstances in the behavior of third parties, in contrast, was real. Yet Cardozo put aside matters that economists would treat as critical to an analysis of market structure and concluded that no changed circumstance, including "the rise of chain stores to affluence and power," altered the balance.[20] Indeed, in his topsy-turvy world, one reason for keeping the meat companies out of the grocery lines of business was that they could provide the goods and services at a lower cost. "When they add groceries to meats, they will do so, they assure us, with substantially no increase of the existing overhead. Thus in the race of competition they will be able by their own admission to lay a handicap on rivals overweighed at the start."[21] Antitrust laws that are designed to spur competition thus become an instrument to suppress it. No wonder the wholesale grocers were out in force.

The substantive deficiencies in Cardozo's decision are compounded by its tough stance on the modification of equitable decrees. Having affirmed the soundness of the provisions of the original decree, Cardozo added that any request for its modification should take place against a background presumption of its initial validity in light of the underlying conditions. Since he found that the "huge size" of the defendants was the dominant operative fact, the changes in market condition took a distinct second place in the analysis, as did concerns with the overall social impact of the decree. As Cardozo put it in an oft-cited passage:

> The inquiry for us is whether the changes are so important that dangers, once substantial, have become attenuated to a shadow. No doubt the defendants will be better off if the injunction is

relaxed, but they are not suffering hardship so extreme and unexpected as to justify us in saying that they are the victims of oppression. Nothing less than a clear showing of grievous wrong evoked by new and unforeseen conditions should lead us to change what was decreed after years of litigation with the consent of all concerned.[22]

The reference to "after years of litigation" seems odd, given that the consent decree was entered on the day the litigation was filed; perhaps Cardozo was thinking of the endless back and forth during the following ten years. But the general statement has significance that goes beyond the particular facts. From start to finish, Cardozo takes the view that those who have consented to lie on a bed of nails must live with the lacerations that follow. In reading his opinion, one is tempted to excuse the shoddy economics on two grounds. The first is that no one knew any better about the situation, and the second is that even if they did, there was little that Cardozo could have done to expand the ability of courts of equity to modify their initial decrees. Both points, however, seem wrong in light of the short and pointed dissent of Justice Butler.

Butler relied on (without reproducing) the extensive findings of fact that had been entered into by the district court, which indicated just how badly the firms had fared under the decree. One formal stipulation in the case, Butler begins, was that all the signatories to the consent decree "are in active competition with each other," so that the facts "negative any suggestion that danger of monopolistic control now exists."[23] He then proceeds to marshal the evidence to show that many of the defendant firms had suffered significant operating losses. One firm sold assets to a second, which in turn could not make a reasonable rate of profit either before or after financing; a third went into receivership. Butler then offers tabular evidence that "the defendants' earnings, whether considered in relation to sales or to the worth of property invested, are low and substantially less than those of others carrying on the same lines of business."[24] One obvious inference is that the decree crippled the firms' operation in ways that advanced no legitimate antitrust objective.

Butler added a further point, glossed over in Cardozo's cavalier account: Chain stores did, indeed, alter consumer behavior by diverting their business from the specialized butchers served by Swift and Armour to larger establishments that carried both groceries and meat products.[25] Due to the decree, Swift and Armour could not adopt for this fast-growing market segment the same economies of scale open to "the integrated firms in strong hands" that were not saddled with the same restrictions. And for whose benefit? Butler's words are as relevant now as then:

> The denial of that relief makes against competition intended to be preserved by the Sherman Anti-Trust Act. Defendants should be permitted more efficiently to use their help and equipment to lessen their operating expenses. That makes for lower prices, and so is in the public interest. . . . The whole-sale grocers, represented here by objecting interveners, are not entitled to the court's protection against the competition of nonmembers or of defendants carrying on separately and competing actively.[26]

Cardozo's "grievous wrong" standard misses all the strong evidence of the counterproductive nature of the decree. But did it have to be such? Not really. As Butler notes, the consent decree stated that "this stipulation shall not constitute or be considered as an admission, and the rendition or entry of the decree, or the decree itself, shall not constitute or be considered as an adjudication that the defendants, or any of them, have in fact violated any law of the United States."[27] The most obvious way to read the quoted words is that the United States should be held to its part of the bargain as well. In part, it obtained the quick consent decree because it agreed that it should not receive res judicata effect. The only inference one could draw is that the "grievous wrong" standard, however relevant in other cases, should not override the explicit terms of the agreement. Exactly what standard it does require is left to the imagination. But none of those differences matters here in the face of the exhaustive finding of facts found at the trial level. Appellate courts should not lightly overturn explicit findings by trial judges with a sound grasp of the underlying economic position in order to magnify the importance of a bloated and unsound decree.

ASCAP-BMI

The saga of the ASCAP-BMI litigation, now sixty-five years old (and count-ing), has recently been the subject of excellent studies, making unnecessary a detailed examination of each leg of the tortuous legal journey.[28] The major legal rulings are listed in table 1. The key players are two performing rights organizations (PROs): the American Society of Composers, Authors, and Publishers (ASCAP), formed in 1914, and Broadcast Music Inc. (BMI), formed in 1939, in part in response to widespread dissatisfaction that some artists (as I shall call them collectively) had with ASCAP's licensing practices.

TABLE 1

SUMMARY OF **ASCAP** AND **BMI** CONSENT DECREE HISTORY

Date	Description
1941	**ASCAP and BMI Consent Decree** • Required that licenses be nonexclusive • Allowed individual member/affiliates to directly contract licenses • Required the PROs to offer program licenses in addition to the blanket licenses
1950	**ASCAP Consent Decree, Amended Final Judgment** • Extended arrangement to television • Regulated rates for television program licenses to make them a real alternative
1966	**BMI Consent Decree** • Adopted provisions of ASCAP consent decree
2000	**ASCAP Second Amended Final Judgment** • Extended AFJ to radio • Included all music by ASCAP members in the rate formula, not just the music provided by ASCAP

SOURCES: Michael A. Einhorn, "Intellectual Property and Antitrust: Music Performing Rights in Broadcasting," *Columbia Journal of Law and the Arts* 24, no. 1 (Summer 2001): 349–68; Noel Hillman, "Intractable Consent: A Legislative Solution to the Problem of Aging Consent Decrees in *United States v. ASCAP* and *United States v. BMI*," *Fordham Intellectual Property, Media and Entertainment Law Journal* 8 (Spring 1998): 733–71.

PROs are indispensable intermediaries between the large number of artists who produce music and the even larger public that wants to hear it. Without a PRO, each artist would have to enter into a direct licensing agreement with each of thousands of consumers. The price for each individual license would in all likelihood be small, especially on a per-play basis. Using a PRO intermediary dramatically reduces the transaction costs. Individual members enter into master agreements with a PRO, which in turn becomes their agent in dealing with end users. The PRO negotiates the fees paid to the PRO, a holdback for administrative expenses, and the allocation of revenues among its members.

The efficiency advantages from using PRO middlemen are illustrated by a simple calculation. In 1979, ASCAP had 22,000 members and BMI had 30,000 members. Today ASCAP boasts over 200,000 members, and BMI over 300,000.[29] If each present member of ASCAP or BMI were to reach out directly to each end user, even with ASCAP's 1979 membership, members would need 2.2 billion contracts to cover this market segment, while for the same year BMI would need 3.0 billion. Today the numbers would be roughly tenfold. The stupendous transaction costs would overwhelm the gains from trade, and the entire industry would massively constrict, as only the major players on either side of the market would be able to afford to hammer out individual deals. Introduce the intermediaries, and now for the 1979 period there are 50,000 contracts between artists and PROs, and 100,000 between PROs and end users. That number is larger today, but the massive reduction in transaction costs remains. And even that reduction of needed contracts by over 99.9 percent understates the gains. Unorganized individual agreements would be chaotic and inconsistent. The PRO can adopt standard form arrangements to streamline transaction costs on both sides of the market.

Unfortunately, the creation of PROs also creates a serious antitrust problem, which in turn leads to tricky judgments on legal enforcement. One way to look at a PRO agreement is to see it as all potential competitors in the market banded together to find one or two agents who will sell their goods—at above-competitive prices. The organization that overcomes the transaction problem to allow communication between the two sides of the market will, of necessity, overcome what would otherwise be an insuperable transaction-cost problem for parties on the *same* side of the market when those parties wish to collude with each other to raise prices and exclude rivals.

As a first approximation, the easiest solution is to take the bitter with the sweet. A finding that horizontal cooperation among PRO members is anticompetitive would doom the organizations from the outset, to the detriment of their customers. Thus, when the issue reared its head, the Supreme Court in *Broadcast Music Inc. v. Columbia Broadcasting System Inc.* (1979) rejected a per se analysis in favor of a more persuasive rule of reason on the ground that PRO arrangements were not "naked" restraints that only served to line the pockets of the PRO's members.[30] Stated otherwise, some form of coordination has to be allowed among PRO members. But that does not answer the further question of what kind of licenses should be allowed. All licenses may not be created equal, and it could be possible to impose restrictions on the different license types in ways that do little to compromise the efficiency gains from coordination, while reducing the potential for monopoly rents.[31] The consent decrees that have been in place in this industry since 1941 are a fair measure of the level of complexity in this area. The evolution of these transactions does not show the same downward spiral observed in *Swift*, but it remains highly doubtful that the Byzantine course of this litigation was in the end worth the candle, given the difficult judgment calls that had to be made countless times along the way.

The saga begins with the original blanket licenses that ASCAP offered for live productions of its covered works in the era before radio. These blanket licenses allowed the use of any and all musical numbers in the ASCAP catalogue for a single fixed fee, which was calibrated with reference to either potential revenue or to the size of the music hall, the number of patrons, or some other measure that positively correlated with the value of the license to its particular user. These rules, which are still in effect today,[32] have evident efficiency features. The effort was to tie pricing to value received by the licensee by avoiding the unhappy result of having a single fixed-dollar fee for all users. While allowing small theaters to gain valuable licenses for their productions, that strategy did not disadvantage the operators of larger establishments who had to pay, more or less, the same amount per patron as their smaller rivals.

The advent of radio opened up a large new market for ASCAP's libraries and presented novel challenges in setting licensing fees, chiefly through blanket licenses that covered the entire portfolio of music for one fixed price. As Michael Einhorn has noted, these arrangements, too, have real efficiency advantages: "Blanket licenses economize on transaction costs, insure against involuntary infringement, and efficiently price each additional performance unit at zero, which is the immediate marginal cost of production."[33] Unfortunately, however, they also have anticompetitive potential. Prior to 1932, ASCAP's fee schedules paid no attention to which songs were played how often. That matter was one for internal allocation of revenues, net of expenses, among its various members. Rather, ASCAP rules tied the size of the fee to the number of broadcast hours for its songs.[34] As in the live-performance market, that is a sensible effort to even out the revenue on a per-customer basis, which marks the competitive ideal. But in 1932, ASCAP changed its practice and set its fees as a percentage of total revenues of the station for its entire broadcast period, whether or not ASCAP material was used in any given segment.

The shift had negative implications for the likelihood of new entry by competitors. Under the pre-1932 scheme, a station was not disadvantaged if it decided to use ASCAP's libraries for part of its programming, while going elsewhere for the rest. Fewer hours of ASCAP music meant lower fees paid. But once the ASCAP fees were tied to annual station revenue, the station received no price break by broadcasting music from other sources. The new pricing arrangement did not enhance ASCAP's ability to discharge its clearinghouse functions—only its ability to exclude rivals from gaining market share, even when they could offer a substitute product of equal quality at a lower price. Under the relentless "all or nothing" logic of the blanket license, the broadcaster received no price reduction by cutting back on the hours that it used ASCAP material, so it had to pay a very high cost for using substitute sources of supply.

This feature of the blanket license spurred the Department of Justice to launch a criminal prosecution of ASCAP in 1934. That prosecution was held in abeyance until 1941, when the department negotiated with ASCAP a consent decree intended to overcome the entry restriction implicit in the blanket license form. ASCAP agreed to offer so-called "program licenses" which allow the broadcaster to acquire at some reduced fee a license for a particular time slot, which in turn would allow it to buy programming for other slots from other sources. BMI, newly formed in 1939, acceded to the same terms in 1941. Both early decrees made it illegal for either ASCAP or

BMI to require exclusive licenses from its licensees or to price-discriminate within particular classes of customers (a feature that ASCAP now promotes as ensuring fairness for its customers). The *nonexclusive* provision in these consent decrees allowed potential licensees to negotiate directly with individual copyright holders so that artists could, in effect, compete against themselves. Wisely, however, the consent decrees did *not* interfere with the established contract rule that barred dual affiliation for any individual artist, who could belong to only one PRO.[35]

There is much to commend in these early settlements. Foremost, they lacked the anticompetitive effect of the original *Swift* decree. Far from blocking new entry into collateral markets, the nonexclusive provisions that applied to ASCAP and BMI tended, if anything, to open up the operation of markets. The provisions are relatively easy to draft and are self-enforcing, so that administrative complications are likely to be kept to a minimum. Nor are the provisions likely to depreciate in value, for it is hard to imagine—and no one has identified—changes in the external market that would make the requirements more onerous over time.

Nonetheless, in at least two respects, judicial intervention proved less successful than one might have hoped. First, the two companies stood in analogous positions to each other, but were not subject at all times to the same rules. The ASCAP decree was modified to cover television in 1950; a similar decree was concluded with BMI only in 1966.[36] BMI was the newer organization, yet it also had the larger membership. Part of the explanation lies in the creation by the 1950 ASCAP settlement of a fee-setting rate court in the Southern District of New York that was charged with resolving licensing disputes.[37] Although BMI entered into a television decree in 1966, it was only subject to rate court provisions as of 1994.[38] The effect was dramatic. According to Einhorn, "BMI's considerable increase in market share in the 1960–1994 period resulted, at least in part, from the fact that ASCAP was fee-regulated while BMI was not."[39] Differential regulation is always unwise in a regime with two direct competitors.

Second, the decision to mandate a distinction between blanket and program licenses opens up the ticklish subject of the relative prices of the two types of licenses. Ever since the initial consent decrees, there have been constant protests that ASCAP and BMI have set the program license fees so high that customers have no choice but to stick with the blanket license. Thus, although the performing right societies are required to provide such a product under the consent decrees, per-program licenses are rarely purchased. In most market segments, the performance rights societies have made such licenses so expensive, the process so cumbersome, and the enforcement actions for inadvertent infringement so frightening, most users who can afford to do so, and even those who can not, simply opt for the blanket license even if it means paying for some things they do not want, do not need, and will never use.[40]

One report of ASCAP's complex weighting formulas observes that these premiums range from 60 to 177 percent of the base-rate figure for blanket licenses.[41] That number seems low: Judge Jon O. Newman of the Second Circuit, addressing the issue in *U.S. v. ASCAP* (1984), found sevenfold differences per unit time between blanket and program licenses for various TV shows.[42]

Judge Newman nonetheless found no per se antitrust violation from the issuance of these blanket licenses. This conclusion in *Buffalo Broadcasting v. ASCAP* (1984) rested on two grounds, one substantive and the other procedural, with sharply different implications. While acknowledging that the obligation to provide the program licenses could not be discharged by inflating prices to the point where the licenses in question would not be realistically available, Judge Newman found that the rate differential was overstated because it was not adjusted to take into account the rate base for the two separate licenses. But his opinion offered no explanation whether the offsets, once made, would account for the vast difference between the two rates. The more potent evidence was that virtually no one took the program licenses, even though there were many stations that did not adopt all-music formats. In effect, a bit of methodological laxity in the Second Circuit allowed ASCAP a free pass on a tough issue.

Judge Newman's procedural point has much more bite. The most sensible way to view the matter is to displace future antitrust actions by resorting to the procedures set out in the 1950 amended final judgment (AFJ), which extended the 1941 ASCAP consent decree to television. It goes without saying that the same rules should govern BMI to preserve competitive parity. But the piecemeal nature of the consent decree process precluded that sensible outcome. In particular, the 1950 AFJ, which bound only ASCAP, contained two provisions of note. The first required ASCAP "to use its best efforts to avoid any discrimination among the respective fees fixed for the various types of licenses which would deprive the licensees or prospective licensees of a genuine choice from among such various types of licenses."[43]

Next, in the event license applicants believe they are being overcharged, the ASCAP decree permitted any applicant for a blanket or program license to apply to the district court for the determination of a "reasonable" fee. In such a proceeding, "the burden of proof shall be on ASCAP to establish the reasonableness of the fee requested by it."[44] But the question is, why go through the antitrust process at all? The more expeditious remedy is just to treat ASCAP (or BMI) as a natural monopoly subject to regulation of the sort introduced under the 1950 AFJ, for which there is no comparative advantage in using a judicial body as opposed to some administrative agency. Nonetheless, within the limits of a consent decree, some sort of rate court is the best that can be achieved.[45]

Quite simply, serious limitations of judicial power—which were later to play a large role in the AT&T breakup—prevented this solution. First, no consent decree can bind strangers to the judgment, so that BMI could not be touched by the 1950 ASCAP settlement. And second, no judicial settlement can order the creation of a separate administrative body without running seriously into separation of powers principles. Ratemaking perforce becomes a judicial function.

How, then, should a court proceed in this setting? One way is to use the differential between blanket and program licensees in the pre-1932 period as a presumptive benchmark today. Once that number sets the range of possibilities, the rates for program licenses can be set by a two-step procedure. First, adopt the same revenue formula that is used with respect to the blanket license: a fixed percentage of revenue during the period in question. The revenue base will depend on advertisement revenues that themselves fluctuate with the time of day and the size and composition of the audience. The formula thus offers a natural updating of rates that takes account of inflation and of the contextual value of the music played, both of which will be constantly updated without further judicial intervention.[46] Second, a further adjustment is needed to cover the higher administrative costs of program licenses in such areas as statistical techniques that the PROs typically use (or at least used until recently) to monitor the performance of their music. This approach follows the regulatory technique of allowing a regulated firm to recover the increased costs associated with providing a consumer with some specialized product, where the overall objective is to keep its rate of return constant regardless of choice of license. In effect, the insistence on genuine choice requires the PRO to present a cost-justification that explains why the program license fee should not be a simple fraction of the blanket license.

The risk that remains in this two-part tariff is that PROs may set their rates for blanket licenses artificially high in order to preserve the favorable rates for the program licenses. This strategy, however, is likely to prove largely self-defeating, because it will lead to a sharp reduction in overall sales, given that the PROs have already made clear what they think their optimal license fees ought to be. In addition, it implies, in a world without collusion, a loss of business to the competing firm. Hence, the best strategy is to develop a benchmark figure for the administrative multiple for the program license and leave matters at that.

A variation of this procedure was, in fact, adopted, albeit belatedly and imperfectly, by Magistrate Michael Dolinger in a 1993 decision dealing with license fees for television.[47] After exhaustive hearings, Dolinger allowed for adjustments in both station size and inflation from his benchmark 1972 rates, which is consistent with sound procedures. But he held that a then existing fourfold multiple for program licenses made that choice wholly illusory. Instead, Dolinger sought to promote revenue equivalence among the two types of licenses. He first noted that a blanket ASCAP licensee typically used its license for about 75 percent of its programming. He deduced that revenue equivalence could be achieved by multiplying the base rate by 1.33, which implies that the fee per minute of airtime of ASCAP material is the same under both types of licenses (1.33/1.00 for the shorter period equals 1/0.75 for the longer one). He then added a 7 percent figure to cover the additional administrative overhead. Thereafter, the base figure was adjusted by mutual consent to include a 10 percent "miniblanket" program license to pick up the commercial music broadcast during the day, so as to avoid, for the advantage of both sides, the need to monitor "content" separately from "commercial" music.

There is no reason why this particular scheme could not have been applied across the board for both companies, for both radio and television, at the time of the first television decree in 1950. The weakness of that decree was that it left too much to the imagination when it could have simply added two provisions that would have improved the system for all sides. The first would have made the remedial rate court hearings the sole remedy for the broadcast licensees in all cases against either PRO, which would have spared both ASCAP and BMI the costly antitrust actions in the ensuing years. The second would have ordered a use of the Dolinger methodology from the outset to ensure the needed parity between blanket and program licenses.

Nonetheless, since the Dolinger ruling only applied to television, the problem with massive differences between blanket and program licenses persisted in radio. That issue was addressed in the second amended final judgment (SAFJ) (2000). There no numbers were selected so that the matter was treated solely as one of principle.[48] More specifically, the SAFJ provided that "ASCAP shall use its best efforts to avoid any discrimination among the various types of licenses offered to any group of similarly situated music users that would deprive those music users of a genuine choice among the various types of licenses offered, or of the benefits of any of those types of licenses." It continued to provide: "For a representative music user, the total license fee for a per-program or per-segment license shall, at the time the license fee is established, approximate the fee for a blanket license."[49]

To make matters worse, the SAFJ licenses also had to make some reckoning of ASCAP music that was *not* acquired through ASCAP but under some other license. On this point it deviated from the Dolinger formula, which had allowed ASCAP to figure out the ratio by looking at *only* the music that is licensed through it, and not ASCAP music that comes from the artist under outside licenses. Hence, if 20 percent of the music played comes under a blanket ASCAP license, then under the Dolinger formula any program license is set at fivefold that base rate, so that the cost per minute of music *supplied through ASCAP* remains equal to its rate under the blanket license. People who are willing to pay more for an ASCAP minute under a blanket license have to pay more under the program license as well.

The SAFJ also adopts the use of a multiple, but its base does not contain only the ASCAP music that comes through ASCAP; it contains all music the licensee receives from ASCAP members, no matter how acquired. Thus, suppose, as before, that 20 percent of the total broadcast content comes through ASCAP, but an additional 30 percent of ASCAP broadcast content comes from outside licenses. Under the SAFJ the program license is for only double the blanket license, because ASCAP is treated as supplying half the music, so that the cost per minute is kept constant only with the twofold fee increase.

The SAFJ is less favorable to ASCAP members than the Dolinger formula.[50] In principle, I believe that the Dolinger formula gives the better estimate of the value ASCAP provides. But the entire discussion has an unreal feature about it: Why should anyone pay even double to get the same rights to perform music? In most contexts, the blanket license will dominate, unless the stakes get higher. Thus, the ability to license separately does matter with the so-called dramatic rights, as when someone wants to broadcast an entire musical by a single composer. But those are outside the ASCAP envelope anyhow. Hence, it looks as though there is a concession in the decree that does not cost the PROs very much, although some empirical evidence is needed to verify this prediction.

In sum, the various ASCAP and BMI decrees went wrong in several ways. First, they did not keep ASCAP and BMI in parity at all times, so that differential regulations governed key portions of their business. Second, they did not institute systematic rate hearings for both organizations, governed by the same principles for both television and radio. Hence, the "genuine choice" issues were never faced systematically head-on, and the blanket license continued to exert more influence than it should have for over half a century. Third, the decrees allowed for antitrust suits to persist when the sound and active administrative remedy would have reduced uncertainty, artificial distinctions between the two competitors, and strategic gamesmanship by individual litigants. If the consent decrees nonetheless avoided serious problems, that is because they conformed, by and large, to the golden rule: Keep consent decrees simple, and tie them to the core violations to which they are directed. The decrees did not affect the PROs' ability to govern their internal businesses, and they did not restrict technical innovations or entry into new markets. So while there were lost opportunities, there were no catastrophic failures.

United Shoe Machinery

The United Shoe Machinery Company was formed in 1899 by the merger of seven independent firms. From the outset, the merger was subject to constant legal challenges by the United States, culminating generations later in an order to break up United Shoe's Beverly Massachusetts plant. That eleventh-hour breakup, which the Supreme Court sustained in 1968,[51] did more than constrain the power of a dominant player in an important market. It resulted in the closure of its major facility—a futile, belated, and ineffectual effort to make a market competitive, long after global entry had eroded United Shoe's position.[52]

Before the First World War, United Shoe's dominant position in the shoe machinery market attracted the attention of the first generation of antitrust enforcers under the Sherman Act. The two opening salvos were *United States v. Winslow* (1913), and shortly thereafter *United States v. United Shoe Corporation* (1918). Both lawsuits attacked the 1899 consolidation as an illegal combination in restraint of trade in violation of section 1 of the Sherman Act. The second suit also attacked United Shoe's leasing arrangements as attempts to monopolize the shoe machinery market in violation of section 2.

In both cases, it was conceded on all sides that the manufacture of shoes was a complex process involving many distinct steps, each of which was covered by different patents, which were controlled in turn by different members of the consolidated group. After noting that the patents covered distinct processes that were *not* in competition with each other, Justice Joseph McKenna, writing in *United Shoe*, concluded that

> we could "see no greater objection to one corporation manufacturing seventy per cent of three noncompeting groups of patented machines collectively used for making a single product than to three corporations making the same proportion of one group each. The disintegration aimed at by the [Sherman Act] does not extend to reducing all manufacture to isolated units of the lowest degree."[53]

Or, as expressed by one of the judges in the court below, "The combination was not unlawful so far as it did no more than put the different groups of noncompeting patented machines into one control."[54] Clearly, the Court recognized that the formation of the single corporation operated primarily as a means to consolidate a set of patents needed to produce the finished product. In modern terms, the merger arrangements operate like a pooling agreement for complementary patents. Probably, and in line with the modern view, the Court would have taken a different view if the patents had been in competition with each other, for then the trappings of a merger could not excuse the horizontal restraint of trade.[55]

Thus far, the import was only that the merger conferred no additional monopoly power. But the case for the merger is stronger: Its constituent parts were all *vertical* in form, so that consolidation eliminated the blockade problems that previously faced shoe manufacturers who had to deal with multiple patent holders. That consideration explicitly entered into the judicial calculation with respect to United Shoe's acquisition of the so-called Plant patents:

> There was no other way out of the deadlock, if the inventions were to be used together—that is, embodied in one machine, without infringement—than by ownership in one hand of all the patents. That plan was adopted and was the inducement of the purchase of the Plant inventions by the United Company.[56]

The Court understood that integration—what we now call the elimination of the "double marginalization" problem—produced transactional *gains* shared by all market participants. And, it found additional efficiencies: The consolidated patent portfolio made it easier to work patent improvements, and the consolidation allowed for the more efficient deployment of labor at the single Beverly factory.[57]

The section 2 analysis in *United Shoe* was more troublesome because it gave a clean bill of health to a range of leasing practices that would face repeated judicial scrutiny in the coming years. The Court found no relevance in the point that the leases generally ran for seventeen years (the full length of the underlying patent), or that they generally did not allow for amendments by the lessee. Furthermore, the Court rejected the government's tying claim against United Shoe's practice "to make it in effect condition of the lease that the lessee shall not use the machines of competitors either to supply a need for additional machines of the kind leased or for machines of other important though wholly different types."[58] The government also protested, again to no avail, against an "exclusive use" clause, discontinued in 1907, whereby United Shoe could cancel the lease of any machinery if it were used in conjunction with that of rivals. (Violation of the provision resulted in the termination of *all* United Shoe leases.)

McKenna's decision dismissed the genuine concern with full-line-forcing with the observation that the lease terms are best understood as "simply bargains," based on the underlying patent rights.[59] A pointed dissent, authored by Justice William R. Day, noted the difficulties with that analysis:

> The necessary effect of these prohibitive provisions, in view of the dominating control of the business by the lessor, is to prevent the lessee from using other similar machines, however advantageous to him it may be to do so, unless he is willing to incur the peril of losing machinery essential to his business. It likewise so curtails the field of free customers as to keep others from manufacturing such machinery. Whenever a new machine is acquired by the lessee for the period of seventeen years (the full life of a patent under the statutes of the United States) the chain is forged anew which binds him to the use of the lessor's machines, to the practical exclusion of all others.
>
> Under the system of leasing, now before us, the patentee not only undertakes to grant the use of the machines covered by the letters patent, but to dictate the supplies with which they shall be used; to compel their surrender if the machine of another is used; to prevent their use except with other machinery furnished by the patentee; to extend the monopoly of the invention beyond the 17 years allowed by the statute; to lease the use of the invention only upon terms which permit the lessor to forfeit the patent license, and to terminate, if he chooses, all similar leases to use the machines of the lessor. And these extraordinary claims of right are made under the grant of the patent which gives to the inventor the exclusive right to make, use, and sell his invention, and nothing more.[60]

As in ASCAP and BMI, the insistence on licensing the whole product line works to exclude others who might wish to compete for sales at some stage of the process. But the case against United Shoe is somewhat weaker than that against the PROs. The use of songs by first one PRO and then another has no negative effects on production. In contrast, as Justice McKenna suggests, the mixing of United Shoe's equipment with that of multiple outsiders surely does. Let something go wrong somewhere along the line, and, owing to the interdependence of the production stages, it could become very difficult to figure out which supplier provided the equipment responsible for the disruption of the process. Whether this justification is strong enough to trump section 2 concerns is, in the absence of empirical evidence, an open question, but the issue should not be waved off.

To his credit, McKenna did not rest his case solely on this grand generalization. He also made explicit efficiency arguments, noting that the array of machines worked better when they were in "proper relation" to each other, available for "instantaneous service" from a common source.[61] The Court even referred to the standard trade-off of antitrust law and observed that the lessees entered into the leases "upon a calculation of their value— the efficiency of the machines balanced against the restrictions upon and conditions of their use."[62] But the Court did not ask the more difficult question whether the efficiency calculus for the lessee tracked the efficiency calculus for society.

United Shoe's victory did not last long, for five years later Justice Day had his revenge against Justice McKenna. In a new suit against United Shoe, the government relied not on the Sherman Act, but, rather, on section 3 of the Clayton Act, which prohibited lease terms whose effect may be to lessen competition substantially or tend to create a monopoly. Making the same arguments as in his previous dissent, Justice Day outlawed the lease restrictions that had been sustained in the earlier case.[63] Naturally, United Shoe objected to this renewed attack as an attempt to relitigate under the Clayton Act the same issues that had been decided five years earlier between the same parties. A bit of nimble footwork allowed Justice Day to hold that the former claim did not preclude bringing the new suit, since the "may lessen competition" standard of the Clayton Act was more favorable to the government than "attempted monopolization" under Sherman Act, section 2.[64]

In similar fashion, Justice Day rejected any argument that the litigation constituted a "taking" of United Shoe's patents because it limited the company's ability to dispose and use its patents as it saw fit, noting that the patentee was held subject to the usual police-power limitations on private property.[65] At this point, the question of patent protection becomes a special instance of the larger question of the overall protection of private property against government regulation. At a minimum the property protections make it impermissible for the United States to strip patent holders of their rights of exclusive use.[66] But it should not make constitutional all restrictions on a patentee's right to use, license, or sell its patent.[67] The most sensible accommodation lets the general antitrust laws prevent an agreement between holders of substitute patents to raise price or restrict outputs. But that view hardly validates every legislative restriction that prevents a patentee from charging market rates for the sale or license of patented materials, or even from selling or licensing them at all. The erratic constitutional protection of intellectual property was evident even in the supposedly pro-property era of the pre–New Deal Court.

With these preliminaries to one side, the case turned to the main antitrust event. Justice Day did not examine whether efficiency arguments that had been made for the lease restrictions negated their adverse competitive effect. Nor did he make any predictions about the impact of the mandated change in leasing provisions on the overall structure of the shoe machinery market or United Shoe's share of that market. His approach treated these leases as virtual per se offenses, which rested on an unstated assumption that once the fetters on competition were removed, the market would sort itself out. After a fashion it did without noticeable change—until, in 1947, the United States initiated the *third* round of litigation against United Shoe Machinery, which resulted over twenty years later in the mandated breakup of its Beverly facility and the rapid demise of the firm.

The initial puzzle about this third-round litigation is why it, too, was not barred by the earlier suits. The answer rests largely on the uneasy way in which the procedural doctrines of finality mesh with ongoing substantive activities. Thus, the earlier litigation did stop the attacks on the initial 1899 consolidation of United Shoe, and it insulated from further review the allegations of wrongdoing that culminated in the 1922 lawsuit. But in the 1947 suit, the government brought charges under sections 1 and 2 of the Sherman Act for actions that took place *after* the 1922 final judgment, and thus rested on a new set of operative facts (to which the doctrine of res judicata, even today, does not apply): United Shoe's acquisitions over the previous twenty-five years, and its general practice of leasing instead of selling its equipment (even stripped of all the clauses found illegal under the 1922 suit). The new action sought

> an injunction against future violations; a cancellation of United's shoe machinery leases; a requirement that United offer for sale all machine types 'manufactured and commercialized by it and be enjoined from leasing shoe machinery except upon terms . . . approved by the Court'; a requirement that, on such terms as the court may deem appropriate, United make available to all applicants all patents and inventions relating to shoe machinery; an injunction against United manufacturing or distributing shoe factory supplies, and a divestiture of United's ownership of virtually all branches and subsidiaries concerned with shoe factory supplies or tanning machinery.[68]

After a long trial, U.S. District Judge Charles E. Wyzanski issued an exhaustive opinion, which was affirmed by the United States Supreme Court in a one sentence *per curiam* opinion.[69] Wyzanski found that United Shoe Machinery had revenues of just over $100 million and profits of around $10 million per annum; that the shoe machinery market was contracting even as shoe production increased; and, most importantly, that United Shoe's market share for most kinds of shoe machinery was well over 90 percent, with a few markets as low as 50 percent and many close to 100 percent. The share of United Shoe's equipment in use followed the same pattern, with, however, a lower market share in certain sublines. On average, it appeared that United Shoe supplied "over 75%, and probably 85%, of the current demand in the American shoe machinery market."[70]

The clear implication was that the invalidation of the earlier lease provisions had had little effect on United Shoe's dominant market position. The explanation can no longer be tied to the perpetuation of earlier discontinued anticompetitive practices, and looks from the outside to be evidence of the quality of United Shoe's equipment and the perceived efficiency, wholly apart from lease provisions, of running an integrated line from a single producer, even if allowed to substitute in alternative equipment at all stages of the production process. In addition, Judge Wyzanski found that the company had a strong research group that accounted for many successful patents, so much so that the government argued (but could not establish) that United's excellence in research, and its overall rate of innovation, should be treated as an effective barrier to entry.[71]

Against this background, it seems clear the divestiture of companies acquired after 1922 would accomplish little to increase competition. As Judge Wyzanski noted, these were few in number and of small dollar amount.[72] Separating these few and small transactions years after they were completed made no economic sense, and could have proved counterproductive, especially if it required equipment users to deal with multiple providers in organizing their lines. There was an evident tendency in the earlier cases to presume a stronger causal connection between the illegal practices and the dominant market position than actually takes place—an easy inference that this natural experiment tends to falsify. Still, the government did treat acquisitions as evidence of market power, which shaped the remainder of its position on United Shoe's leases post-1922. The government objected to four clauses that survived the 1922 final judgment:

> (a) the period of time—[ten years]—covered by the lease, that is, its term, (b) the requirement that a lessee of a unit charge machine should pay a monthly minimum charge, (c) the requirement that such lessee shall use his machine to its full capacity, and (d) the obligation of the lessee at the termination of the lease to make a deferred payment or return charge.[73]

The government then proposed four types of remedies: dissolution, and restrictions on lease terms, supply activities, and patents.

Dissolution. Judge Wyzanski showed little patience with the government's proposal to dissolve United into three separate manufacturing companies, calling it unrealistic:

> United conducts all machine manufacture at one plant in Beverly, with one set of jigs and tools, one foundry, one laboratory for

machinery problems, one managerial staff, and one labor force. It takes no Solomon to see that this organism cannot be cut into three equal and viable parts.

Nor can the division of United's business be fairly accomplished by dividing the manufacture of machinery into three broad categories, and then issuing an injunction restraining the Beverly plant from manufacturing two broad categories of machine types, and vesting in each of two new companies the right to manufacture one of those categories. Such an order would create for the new companies the most serious type of problems respecting the acquisition of physical equipment, the raising of new capital, the allotment of managerial and labor forces, and so forth. The prospect of creating three factories where one grew before has not been thought through by its proponents.[74]

The point seems so persuasive that it requires little comment. The remedy is far more drastic than the underlying offense.

Lease Terms. The simplest approach here is to exclude from the leases those terms that were found to be offending, just as was done in the 1922 judgment. That solution keeps the remedy in line with the underlying violation. But there is, a priori, no reason to think that this remedy could pack any punch. Virtually all the terms—minimum terms, down payments, and refunds—are found in ordinary commercial leases among parties that do not have a particle of market power. The invalidation of the far tougher clauses in the 1922 decree had little impact on market behavior—most probably because the efficiencies of the existing business practices were such that behaviors did not change much even when the clauses were eliminated. Why should the invalidation of the second, far more routine set of terms make much of a dent in United's market share? Or improve social welfare? Having a single supplier to fix all machines with a shop, for example, is a benefit that many firms would desire even if they were not bound to do so by contract.[75] History tends to bear out Justice McKenna's 1918 judgment that these clauses had little restrictive impact and perhaps by stabilizing expectations, had some efficiency gains. Only the full-capacity clause might have some restrictive effect, but even there it is hard to see why a firm would *not* want to use a machine to its full capacity even in the absence of the clause. Under a rule of reason format, restrictions on these lease terms seem sorely wanting.

At this juncture, the court succumbed to the dangerous temptation that marred the consent decree in *Swift & Co.*: impose remedies that go beyond the violation. Judge Wyzanski held that lease terms should be restricted to five-year maximums and early return rights should be guaranteed to users.[76] Obviously, the users gain flexibility, but to what end? If the required terms were mutually beneficial, we should expect to see them in any event. If not, the restraint on contractual freedom is likely to burden both parties to the transaction, and so would disappear over time. It is not clear that the option is valuable to begin with, or, if it is, that it is worth the probable price increase. The antitrust gain from letting in new parties before the expiration of the longer lease seems tenuous at best. Yet, oddly, Judge Wyzanski did not take the path that he was to adopt with sales, namely, to require that United Shoe offer the five-year option, while allowing it to continue its standard leases for customers who preferred them.

Not content with placing fresh limitations on the leasing provisions, Judge Wyzanski also mandated a sale alternative. His theory was that once the shoe manufacturers owned their equipment, they could sell it off in order to fund the early purchase of other equipment that they preferred. Sensibly, the judge did not *mandate* sales to the exclusion of leases, given the likely dislocations for manufacturers with limited access to capital markets. But he insisted that if United Shoe "chooses to continue to lease any machine type, it must offer that type of machine also for sale."[77] Judge Wyzanski imposed this remedy because he regarded the leasing system as the third pillar of United Shoe's success, along with its 1899 merger and superior products.[78] To counter the lease's power, the buyer could determine the form of the transactions (subject to the prohibition against ten-year leases). This would "gradually diminish the magnetic hold" that United Shoe had on the marketplace.

While Judge Wyzanski thought sales would allow some manufacturers to dispose of machines that they owned in order to purchase new machines from a competitor, the economics suggest that any such change would have at most small impact on the overall market. The difference between sales and leases is unimportant for equipment that has an expected lifespan about the length of the underlying lease. Resale could only be for scrap value, which in present value terms is negligible. In addition, the sales transaction could have the disadvantage of requiring the new buyer to get third-party financing, which is not necessary in lease transactions, where the lessor plays both a business and a financing role. If the sales transactions are on balance less efficient than the leases, antitrust law will disrupt ordinary business patterns.

A second objection to this approach is similar to the problem that arose in policing the program licenses in the ASCAP and BMI cases. In order for sales (or short-term leases) to count as a "genuine option," there must be some assurance that the terms are financially at least as good as those for the leases. Yet there is little reason for a court to convert itself into a de facto ratemaking agency for a wide range of leases. In order to finesse that possibility, the Court opened up—in ways that were to prove crucial—its long-term hold over the case. Initially, it would allow the parties to sort out the arrangements. But if a lessee thought that a particular item was priced not to sell, it could lodge a protest before the Court. This is better than a system of prior-rate approval—but worse than a system that dispenses with all ratemaking procedures. That was a viable option in *United Shoe*; unlike the ASCAP and BMI situations, there was no close analogy here to the program license that could drive sensible equipment manufacturers to the short-term options.

Supply Activities. The court ordered United Shoe's supply activities, which constituted only a small fraction of its business, sold off, believing that the efficiency losses from their divestiture would be small because they were not fully integrated into the firm's operation.[79] Judge Wyzanski never made clear why that order would do much to counter the monopoly power that did inhere in the firm's integrated activities—which he was *not* prepared to dissolve. In his mind, the spin-off would lead other firms to fill the gap (which is surely true, lest all equipment gather dust on the workplace floor). But, again, the ability to achieve vertical efficiencies through integrated operations probably meant that the remedy cost more than it was worth.

Patent Licensing. Last, the Court imposed a compulsory licensing system on United for its patents. The first objection to this move is by now familiar: Do not apply a remedy to practices whose legality has not been successfully attacked in the underlying litigation. The high level of innovation by United Shoe should be regarded as one of its successes and, if anything, tells us that firms with some monopoly power retain the willingness to innovate. The record did not reveal any reluctance on United Shoe's part to make license deals with others, given that these were an additional source of revenue. Meanwhile, the remedy introduced two major dislocations, both common to compulsory licensing schemes.[80] First, improper rates can distort the initial incentive to invent. The patent system guarantees exclusive rights to allow the inventor to internalize enough of the gains from invention to hasten the process. Once the gains have to be shared with outsiders, the level of innovation will be reduced. Second, a compulsory system introduces administrative costs that erode the profit base. Someone has to determine the appropriate rates and adjust them to the different types of licenses that are offered. This task shares the familiar difficulties of ratemaking for performing rights organizations and for other regulated industries. When subject to political pressure, the chosen figures can vary all over the map. They can be set so high that no one relies on these licenses at all, or so low that no one has an incentive to enter the voluntary market.

Judge Wyzanski's intermediate position was to let the market work until someone protested. But the systematic uncertainty creates real problems, not the least of which is that the patentee cannot choose the parties with whom it does business, or limit the number of parties to whom these licenses issue. As a matter of first principle, these compulsory licenses are a state-initiated taking for which, as in other contexts, just compensation that leaves the patent holder as well off after the imposition as before should be required. We have no information on how this particular program worked out, but we do know that these compulsory programs are widely resisted in other industries, largely on the ground that voluntary transactions will lead to superior outcomes. Whatever market power United Shoe had in the domestic industry, it could not preclude rivals, domestic and foreign, from entering the equipment market.

—ഝ—

Predictably, the decree ordered by Judge Wyzanski and rubberstamped by the United States Supreme Court had no marked effect on the overall structure of the market. Matters came to a head when the Justice Department, as required under the original consent decree, brought the case back before Judge Wyzanski for a decennial review in January 1965. The government did not suggest that the original decree was unnecessary because its restrictions had had so little impact on market structure. Rather, it argued that the earlier remedial efforts had been a failure because "workable competition had not been established."[81] In line with its faulty diagnosis, the government urged that United's business be reconstituted so as to form two fully competing companies in the shoe machinery market. In a thoughtful opinion, Judge Wyzanski rejected that proposal on the ground that the steady erosion of United Shoe's market share—down to about 63 percent from its previous 75–85 percent level—suggested that the decree was slowly doing its job. It is not likely that most of the decline came from the injunction on the leasing terms. Some of it may have come from the costs of constant supervision or, perhaps, from the compulsory licenses that reduced the value of the patents. Alternatively, the decline in market share could easily have resulted from the long-term debilitation of a firm under constant antitrust bombardment. Whatever the empirics may be, though, Wyzanski rightly read *Swift & Co.* to mean that the government was bound by antitrust decrees in the same manner as private parties.

The Supreme Court took a different view. The technical issue before the Court was whether "the grievous wrong" standard of *Swift & Co.* applied in this case, such that the government could have its way only if it offered a clear showing of changed circumstances. The Court was right to downplay any difference between consent decrees and final judgments, for their effect is the same regardless of the path taken. But that does not answer the question of whether both final judgments and consent decrees should be treated as two-way streets, such that the strict *Swift* standard bound the government to the same degree as the antitrust defendant. The Court's short answer was that the government had to be allowed greater latitude: So long as the government could claim that the objectives of the earlier decree had not been achieved in a timely fashion, it could demand a more potent remedy. In this case, to be sure, the original decree required an update of the situation during the first ten years of its enforcement. Hence it could be said that the government was authorized to seek changes, once it had established that the milder means had not taken their desired effect. But the Court stressed that the scope for revision did not depend on that factor:

> If the decree had . . . been silent as to the time for submitting reports and, if necessary, petitions for modification—and if after 10 years it were shown that the decree had not achieved the adequate relief to which the Government is entitled in a § 2 case, it would have been the duty of the court to modify the decree so as to assure the complete extirpation of the illegal monopoly.[82]

Unfortunately, complete extirpation often comes at a very high price. Antitrust decrees will generally make less sense ten years after they are entered than at the time they were first put into place. Hence, the government should have to bear a heavy burden to explain the strong necessity for a tougher set of restrictions. It should be required at the very least to answer the objections to the dissolution raised by Judge Wyzanski the first time around. Those objections were not time sensitive, but relied on the point that divided ownership of the Beverly plant would bring production to a screeching halt. Why that price had to be paid after United Shoe had already been weakened is hard to see.

Nonetheless, when the case went back to Judge Wyzanski in 1969, he ordered the breakup that the government had demanded. He issued no findings as to why that was necessary, and he piled on conditions that limited United Shoe's ability to rely on foreign manufacture to pick up the slack.[83] And so, soon after the 1969 divestiture and decline in the shoe industry, United Shoe was sold to another company.[84] Of course, it could have died a natural death as a result of the foreign competition. But even that unhappy fate would have been preferable to the slow bloodletting under the antitrust laws. Under competition the best party wins. Under an antitrust decree, the heavy hand of the law can destroy a wholly viable competitor.

To this day, scholars disagree on the underlying question of liability. Some argue that virtually all the lease clauses were anticompetitive: United Shoe's strategy was to divide its gains with its lessees, who also stood to gain from entry restriction in the shoe manufacturing business.[85] A rival view insists that the lease provisions were efficient because they offered a viable alternative to numerous and overlapping contractual warranties for the equipment.[86] Nothing makes these two explanations mutually exclusive. In section 2 monopolization cases, the practices under attack are often an amalgam of restrictive practices and efficient contracting, where it is well-nigh impossible to disentangle good from bad effects. The hard but inescapable question is which effects are more dominant.

My own view is to hold back on antitrust enforcement unless there is clear evidence that the restrictive practices dominate the efficiency result. But for remedial purposes, it hardly matters whether that view is right or wrong. Once the antitrust violation had been established, the proper approach was to knock out the offending lease clauses and call it a day. That decision would have allowed United Shoe to adapt to its competitive environment without having to run a constant antitrust gauntlet. It would have left the firm with full patent protection and thus the incentive to innovate, which might have allowed it to meet the foreign competition.

In section 2 cases, uneasiness arises from asking how monopolies are achieved. Those that arise from excellence and innovation should not be subject to legal harassment, while those that do not should be subject to extra scrutiny. That has been the law since Judge Learned Hand's famous decision in the *Alcoa* case, which noted that Alcoa "may not have achieved monopoly; monopoly may have been thrust upon it."[87] Unfortunately, most cases involve a bit of both. The saga of *United Shoe* teaches that we should be wary of a remedial zeal that saps creative juices in seeking to control monopoly risks.

3

The Breakup of the Bell System

The most important set of antitrust consent decrees ever concluded dealt with the regulation and eventual breakup of the former Bell System. Between 1914 and 1982, that system suffered three successive major consent decrees, all based on tenuous monopolization theories, and interspersed with much legal skirmishing. The high points illustrate the dangers of excessive judicial intervention and of the slippage between wrong and remedy.

Ma Bell: Early History

The first Bell System consent decree arose out of a government antitrust suit brought in 1913, at the outset of the Wilson administration, that sought to block Bell acquisition of a small long-distance company in Oregon. The targeted acquisition was part of a consistent plan whereby Bell used its dominant position in the long-distance market to obtain control over local exchange markets by denying all non-Bell local exchanges access to the Bell long-distance network. That strategy allowed local Bell affiliates to offer comprehensive services that no rival local exchange carrier could supply. The 1914 consent decree blocked those exclusive-dealing provisions by requiring the Bell System to grant hookups to other carriers on the same terms that were made available to its Bell affiliates. So far, so good. In fact, the decree can be faulted because it did not do enough to promote competition:

> Local exchange monopolies were left intact, utterly free to continue to refuse interconnection to other local exchange companies. Bell's monopoly long-distance service was reinforced; Bell would be required to interconnect with all local exchanges, but

there was no provision for any competition—or interconnection—among long-distance carriers. Western Union was indeed spun off, but only to provide telegraphy, not telephony.[1]

If the structural features of the decree were insufficient, its administration proved no better. The Justice Department routinely approved Bell System acquisitions until Congress passed the Willis-Graham Act that gave the Interstate Commerce Commission (ICC) (from which the Federal Communications Commission (FCC) was eventually broken off) the power to exempt telephone company mergers and acquisitions from the purview of the antitrust laws.[2] This first round ended with antitrust law taking a back seat to direct regulation.

In 1949, the Truman administration launched the second major antitrust assault against the Bell System. Relying on a mishmash of theories, the government alleged that Bell engaged in anticompetitive behavior by "eliminating competing manufacturers through acquisitions and termination of purchasing contracts." The government also recited a variety of more dubious offenses, including "the predatory accumulation and exploitation of patents"[3] and the sins of excessive wealth and market power. As in the earlier case, structural changes were key to the government's effort to break down the close working relationships among Bell entities. Western Electric would no longer function as the exclusive service arm to the Bell System. At the same time, the Bell Operating Companies would purchase their equipment through competitive bidding, so that both sides of the Bell family would have extensive dealings with third parties that would provide an external check on their clubby relationship. The stranglehold from Bell Labs would be countered by requiring Bell to license its patents to competitors for reasonable royalties on a nondiscriminatory basis, subject to judicial oversight.

The most striking feature of the government's case lies in its remedial choices. As already noted, compulsory licenses compromise innovation by forcing the patentee to go into competition with itself. The original patent bargain starts from the premise that exclusive rights pay for themselves through rapid innovation. Antitrust law should not be allowed to reverse that presumption by requiring a successful innovator to give aid and comfort to its competitors. The forced arrangements between the Bell System and outside firms could also reduce Bell's gains to innovation. None of these remedies, however, made a dent in Bell's monopoly position, held first through its local operating companies and then through its stranglehold on long distance. Nonetheless, after seven years in the wilderness, a 1956 "final judgment" mandated the sharing of patents and related manufacturing know-how. In addition, the decree provided that the Bell System would not enter any business "other than the furnishing of common carrier communications services," with an exception for work for the federal government.

Even though the 1956 decree did little to break up or constrain the monopoly power of the Bell System, it did not operate in a vacuum. The FCC and state regulatory commissions continued to exercise oversight of the Bell System. The successes or failures of that system—and there were many successes—may be attributable to this regulatory oversight or to the excellence of the Bell management in running and upgrading its system. The antitrust element played too small a role to really matter. The only significant litigation under the 1956 decree arose on a topic that would loom large in the ensuing years: what kinds of activities counted as "common carrier communications services"? While the term suggests that any service used to transmit voice or data over wire should count, it was an open question whether it encompassed certain forms of "enhanced services," including data processing services. The FCC held that it did. But while the line-of-business restrictions in the 1956 decree shielded the Bell System from competition, the proliferation of new technologies exacted an ever-higher price: New forms of business that fit well with traditional forms of telephony could be left outside the ambit of the exclusive grant. Yet it is unclear who, aside from enterprising competitors, benefited from these restrictions. That real defect aside, much can be said for the 1956 final judgment; due to its lack of ambition, it did little harm. Alas, that cannot be said of the ambitious 1982 consent decree that broke up the Bell System.

The 1982 Consent Decree

The Ford administration filed the government's third antitrust action in November 1974, alleging that the Bell System had engaged in illegal monopolization of the telecommunications industry. The ensuing breakup of the Bell System made the government breakup of the Beverly Plant in

United Shoe look like chump change. Instead of dismembering a single successful factory, Judge Harold H. Greene (who had been assigned to the case in 1978) dismembered the vaunted Bell System into what eventually became seven Bell Operating Companies (BOCs)—each with its own geographic base—and one long-distance company, the truncated AT&T. Judge Greene should receive neither the full credit nor the full blame. The 1982 decree came during the Reagan administration and was driven on the government side by the assistant attorney general for antitrust, William Baxter, a Stanford Law professor and distinguished promarket antitrust scholar, who worked tirelessly for the breakup. For all their differences, both Greene and Baxter shared the belief that ongoing regulation of the Bell System was ineffective against a large and skilled integrated firm. And so, "in an April 1981 press conference, Bill vowed to litigate the case 'to the eyeballs'" which, true to his word, he did.[4]

The combination of a single-minded academic and a willful judge proved too much for even the AT&T lawyers to overcome, and the basic decree was struck on the terms that Baxter advocated and Greene embraced. Judge Greene's decree gave each BOC an exclusive monopoly as the local exchange carrier (LEC) in its territory, and obliged each to supply all long-distance carriers with equal and appropriate interconnections, subject to rate regulation by the FCC. The service prohibitions reflected Judge Greene's acceptance of the basic Baxter fear that each BOC could use its control over its own local exchange to discriminate against other long-distance carriers.[5] The decree also forbade the BOCs from entering any other line of telephone business, including competitive long-distance service and forays into the information services and equipment businesses, although it did not explain why each BOC had to be prohibited from entering the long-distance market *outside* its own local service area. The prohibition against manufacturing equipment stemmed from the concern that the BOCs would pad their costs in order to increase their rates under regulation.[6]

On the other end of the divestiture, AT&T was to operate exclusively in the long-distance market, which would be open to competition from new carriers. Baxter had, for example, taken the position that "AT&T's control over the natural monopoly segment of the industry, local exchange service, had placed it in the position to leverage its power into other industry segments which depended on the local exchange network."[7] In his view, that threat was multifaceted because without the separation, AT&T could take advantage of that position by way of self-dealing and cross-subsidization, both of which would systematically discriminate against and disadvantage outside competitors.

The 1956 final judgment, with its line of business restrictions, was vacated in its entirety and replaced by the 1982 consent decree, which allowed AT&T to participate fully in competitive activities, including the provision of information services. (Judge Greene rightly argued that AT&T's attempts to discriminate in favor of its own services would be thwarted by market competition.) The only restriction on AT&T was that it could not reacquire any of the BOCs. Baxter, as a political figure, departed from the scene shortly after the decree was adopted. In contrast, Judge Greene remained active in the case until it was superseded by the 1996 Telecommunications Act. Greene, who died in 2000, could not have foreseen that one of the BOCs (Southwestern Bell) would, after a successful career of acquisitions, acquire the remains of AT&T and promptly rename itself—AT&T.

During his fourteen-year reign, Judge Greene exercised a steely impartiality in his massive decree. The full history has been set out in painful detail by Michael Kellogg, John Thorne, and Peter Huber;[8] my more modest purpose is to examine how the Bell decree stacked up against its stated purpose of improving competitive conditions in the telecommunications industry. While any judgment is difficult because the relevant variables are so numerous and interdependent, a fair assessment is that the decree suffered from an excess of ambition and from a lack of focus and finitude. A man of immense energy and ability, Judge Greene failed to realize that even he could not control the unruly set of forces his divestiture program helped set in motion.

The task of the Bell consent decree was especially daunting because communications is a network industry, regulated by the Federal Communications Commission. That simple observation points to three salient problems: the lack of a clear competitive solution; the difficulty of coordinating multiple regulators; and the complexity of administering an intricate system of cross-subsidies.

No Competitive Solution. The broad objectives of antitrust law—to prevent the creation of monopoly and preserve and maintain competitive conditions—are not attainable in network industries. For the telephone system to work as a system, each user has to be able to link up with all other users. That condition in turn requires either an integrated network with a single supplier, or state oversight to overcome the negotiation and coordination problems that block complete interconnection. Interestingly, it appeared that Baxter himself never quite grasped that crucial point. To be sure, Baxter was ever alert to the dangers that remained so long as AT&T was an integrated company. But he demonstrated no awareness of the new risks that the 1982 consent decree could introduce. Thinking globally, Baxter, like all strong market economists, always stressed the importance of trade-offs in the operation of complex social institutions. Yet he did not show any real caution on this matter, even though it should have been evident even then that the breakup of AT&T did not, and could not, usher in a golden age of pure competition.

Baxter's error surely influenced Judge Greene's approach. Greene's thinking moved between the poles of ineffective regulation and true competition. "There has long been a debate," Greene wrote,

> over the relative merits of regulation and competition. The evidence adduced during the *AT&T* trial indicates that the Bell System has been neither effectively regulated nor fully subjected to true competition. The FCC officials themselves acknowledge that their regulation has been woefully inadequate to cope with a company of AT&T's scope, wealth, and power.[9]

As we will see, Judge Greene's own scheme, which explicitly relied on the FCC to set access charges, was best described as a supplement to a system of regulation already entrusted to a "woefully inadequate" FCC.

The successful integration of multiple firms in network industries is made exceedingly difficult by the intrinsic imbalance among multiple firms with different-sized customer bases. In these settings, mandated interconnections offer a systematic gain to the smaller firm. They gain access to millions of accounts for their customers but need to grant larger firms access to only thousands of accounts. That dynamic derails most voluntary negotiations, as large firms would rather starve out than cooperate with their upstart competitors. Since everyone has to deal with everyone else, an increase in the number of parties does *not* mean more options; it means more chokeholds. Some form of state intervention becomes necessary to forge interconnection.

The problem has no competitive solution, as that term is traditionally understood. There are only different modes of industry coordination or amalgamation, each of which necessarily falls short of the competitive ideal. While a single integrated system has scads of monopoly power, multiple separate systems can each have monopoly power in their exclusive territories. Fragmentation therefore requires forced cooperation between firms, which is not part of any standard antitrust regime. Judge Greene, however, failed to recognize that a clean transformation from monopoly to competition was not in the cards. The relevant question was whether his new industry structure generated more benefits than costs.

Since the Bell System was already up and running, the right approach should have considered three cost factors: the administrative costs in running the consent decree; the mistakes in design and execution from the new system (which are likely to exceed the cost of keeping an existing system on track); and the added uncertainty costs of the breakup—which will adversely affect the investment decisions not only of the old components of the Bell System, but also of newer competitors and suppliers. The breakup of the Bell System could not have been justified merely by showing that the broken-up phone system runs, either in a static or dynamic sense, better than the previous integrated system. Even that seems doubtful, but the hefty transition costs matter as well. Judge Greene ignored these variables, as did Baxter.

Multiple-Track Regulation. Judge Greene could not fully administer the new system that he created. The BOCs had to forge interconnections with AT&T and other long-line carriers which could not be negotiated voluntarily. Hence, the Bell decree necessarily expanded the number and difficulty of the ratemaking procedures within the FCC. From the get-go, the consent decree introduced a third layer of regulation on top of a system that already divided regulatory authority between the FCC and the various state commissions. Judge Greene was aware of this risk, but moved firmly ahead down the divestiture track. In so doing, he brushed aside weighty constitutional and statutory objections.

One set of issues concerns federal-state relationships, where Judge Greene gave the whip hand to the federal government. He held that the state commissions always came out second in a system that is predicated on the supremacy of the federal government on all matters that fall within the scope of federal power.[10] No explicit federal law, however, called for the breakup of the Bell System. It is far from clear that the supremacy clause privileges a judicial action predicated on the Sherman Act, especially since Congress had designed a regulatory structure that reserved a distinct role for state commissions. Still—shades of *United Shoe*—the Supreme Court affirmed Judge Greene's decree without opinion, notwithstanding the size of the case and the trickiness of its structural constitutional issues. Only Justice William Rehnquist's lone dissent expressed concern over "the notion that a district court, by entering what is in essence a private agreement between parties to a lawsuit, invokes the Supremacy Clause powers of the Federal Government to pre-empt state regulatory laws."[11]

On a second issue, Judge Greene concluded, dubiously, that Congress had no intention to let the Communications Act of 1934 override the Sherman Act. Judge Greene should have been more uneasy about using a general federal statute with an immense reach to override another *federal* law that covers a particular portion of this vast field with the same objective—namely, the effort to curb monopoly power of the regulated industry. Why would Congress undermine its own elaborate and exhaustive administrative communications scheme, which could be accused of error but hardly, in light of its extensive regulatory role, of inaction? Judge Greene held repeatedly that "regulation under the Communications Act is neither sufficiently explicit nor sufficiently pervasive to allow it to stand in the way of the enforcement of the antitrust laws."[12] The far better view, however, is that the active operation of the FCC and of state commissions occupies the field.

Indeed, Judge Greene himself later noted that his judicial divestiture needed to receive FCC approval by statute.[13] On this occasion, the FCC agreed with Judge Greene, but judicial power must respond less to the FCC administrative position and more to the structure and design of the statute. The FCC should not have been allowed to use its strategic assent to bypass the long and protracted administrative procedures that it would have had to undertake to bring about the AT&T breakup on its own.

Nor, ironically, did the consent decree remove the FCC from the picture after the breakup was implemented. Only the FCC, not Judge Greene, could set the rates needed to administer the new interconnection system. Judge Greene suspected the BOCs would discriminate in favor of their former owner, which is why the original decree provided that "each BOC shall begin to offer to all interexchange carriers exchange access on an unbundled, tariffed basis, that is equal in type and quality to that provided for the interexchange telecommunications services of AT&T and its affiliates."[14] It is as though Judge Greene thought that after breakup members of the old Bell family would work together covertly to keep outsiders from poaching their markets. His decree shows no awareness of the donnybrooks to come.

Judge Greene imposed several conditions that the government had not requested. He allowed the BOCs, if appropriate, to recover by 1994 certain expenses from AT&T for implementing the equal access provision of the decree; reserved the Bell name to the BOCs (for use in combination, such as Bell Atlantic), to the exclusion of AT&T; required AT&T to issue BOCs (but not other competitors, who were only protected by the interchange rules) royalty-free licenses for existing AT&T patents; allowed the BOCs to construct or maintain facilities to conduct their internal operations; prohibited BOCs from providing interchange-writing, order-typing, or other services exclusively for AT&T; and required AT&T and the BOCs to continue to bargain in good faith with their respective unions. (The last provision served to bar the companies from avoiding successor liability on preexisting union contracts.)[15] Again, only Justice Rehnquist thought that this assertion of judicial power raised serious separation of powers issues.[16] He surely had a point: It is far from clear that a judge should be able to require the executive branch to accept forms of relief that it did not request.

Subsidies. Generally, competitive industries will bleed out subsidies to any identifiable class of users. Customers asked to pay the subsidy as a condition of doing business with a particular firm will migrate to one of its competitors. Some regulatory device is needed to counteract this powerful tendency. The problem is of heightened importance in telecom because of its bewildering array of embedded subsidies: minimum service for poor people, and preference for residential over commercial users, for rural over urban users, and for local phone service over long-distance. This last subsidy is particularly costly because the high elasticity of demand for long-distance calls suggests that most of the joint costs of the system should be charged to local users, where the elasticity is much lower.[17] One advantage of the old Bell System was that the FCC and state commissions could use their regulatory power to provide for a stable system of subsidies. Within an integrated system one can price some services above competitive levels in order to offset the losses incurred by pricing other services below those levels. Once the Bell System was broken up, it became far more difficult to preserve the subsidies.

One possibility was to charge the new AT&T access fees above marginal costs to fund the preferred services and clientele. But this approach creates serious difficulties unless like charges are imposed on new competitors who are not parties to, and hence not subject to, the consent decree. Judge Greene's decree, therefore, necessarily distorted the relationship AT&T had with its carriers. Because neither the Congress nor the FCC wanted a spike in the cost of local phone services, the die was cast. As Paul MacIvoy and Kenneth Robinson wrote in 1985, "Local rates continue to be subsidized while BOC revenue requirements are supplemented by non-cost-based access charges levied on AT&T and the Other Common Carriers (OCCs)."[18]

Note how the situation had turned. Baxter had foreseen only the difficulties that could arise when firms set their internal purchase prices. He did not see the risk that high rates of interconnection could create transfer payments through regulation. AT&T may have started out as the party to watch, but throughout the process it was always hampered by the heavy burdens of regulation, especially in relationship to other long-distance carriers, which were not bound by the decree. Consistent with this view, MacIvoy and Robinson believed that AT&T came out the loser under the consent decree, even though it was freed of the line-of-business restrictions.[19]

Matters were made worse because only AT&T was bound by the consent decree and thus subject to unique regulatory burdens. Judge Greene acknowledged this point in explaining why he would not prevent AT&T or other long-distance carriers from bypassing the BOCs should technology allow for it.[20] His view was that the imbalances between AT&T and the OCCs should be taken care of by future legislation, not by "Luddite" measures that stopped all technical advances. He was clearly right on the need of addressing the problem of universal service in a world with multiple phone companies, but far too optimistic on the odds of solving it. For what it is worth, the differential impact of the Universal Service Obligation continued through the 1996 Telecommunications Act, which took as a given the industry structure of the 1982 consent decree until a host of mergers and new entrants upset the original balance.

—ᴍ—

Judge Greene used monopolization theory to justify a finding of liability against the Bell System. As in the earlier case studies, many of the elements of this charge involved exclusive-dealing practices that could have been banned without ordering a breakup. For example, Judge Greene was persuaded that AT&T had frustrated competitive entry by allowing for interconnection only if the customer had switching equipment both where the call originated and where it terminated. Thus, a customer with a sole office in St. Louis who made a call to Bethesda through Chicago could not use a competitor to AT&T for the first leg of the trip and AT&T for the second, because the customer did not have a Chicago office. In addition, AT&T did not allow for foreign-exchange service, which would have allowed customers to receive local calls through a distant switching center.

Judge Greene rejected Bell's argument that these practices were needed to prevent "cream-skimming," whereby all the cheap calls on high-volume lines would be removed from its network, saddling it with the most expensive calls. In his view, Bell should have met the competitive rates by "de-averaging" its costs. (He did not explicitly consider how this delicate task could be done so long as Bell was required to run cross-subsidies for residential calls through its system, for which a proportionate tax on all carriers is probably the best solution.) Similarly, AT&T insisted that all competitors use expensive "protective connecting arrangements" before hooking their equipment up to Bell's network. Bell purported to justify this practice as a protection of network integrity against physical harm. Judge Greene rightly held that these precautions were excessive relative to the risk and amounted to de facto barriers to entry.[21]

The sensible response would have been to facilitate new competition at the edges of the Bell System by outlawing discrete, identified contractual provisions and business practices, analogous to the limitation on exclusive-dealing provisions in the early stages of *United Shoe Machinery*. Entry through sound interconnection rules is the best countermeasure against monopoly power.[22] Unlike the invalidation of particular contractual terms, entry does change the shape of the market. Competitors could then chip away at the Bell network. Additional orders could have required new entrants to contribute some fraction of their revenue to a universal service fund to maintain whatever cross-subsidies were thought appropriate. In the end, sustained competition would have reduced the size of the Bell System without the wrench of a massive reorganization.

Judge Greene, however, did not rest his decree solely on these discrete practices. Rather, he insisted that the antitrust laws have two objectives: to preserve competition, and to curb those great aggregations of capital that pose a threat to the integrity of the political system. The Sherman Act, Greene maintained, "is founded on a theory of hostility to the concentration in private hands of power so great that only a government of the people should have it."[23]

From that view, narrow remedies are indeed inadequate. But that raises the question why the Bell System had not behaved more insidiously than the record tended to suggest: some possible antitrust violations coupled with an impressive record of technological innovation. Judge Greene's answer was that laudable self-restraint could disappear tomorrow: "The men and women who have guided the Bell System appear by and large to have been careful not to take advantage of its central position in America's economic life. There is no guarantee, however, that future managers will be equally careful."[24]

Indeed, the judge feared that the Bell System might gain control of public debate. "One may speculate, for example, on the effect on the political life of this nation if a company or group with strong political or ideological opinions were to gain effective control of the present Bell System (particularly if the company, additionally, were not precluded from entry into information and electronic publishing services)."[25] Yet at no point did he explain why past and current managers behaved as they did, and for so long; why political institutions offered only feeble guarantees of their own long-term probity; why it didn't make sense to wait for signs of serious misconduct before imposing a major structural change; or why antitrust law should work better than direct regulation to achieve his political goal.[26] In Judge Greene's view, industrial concentration and anticompetitive behavior were so closely entwined that under the public interest provisions of the Tunney Act only divestiture could root out the antitrust violations he had identified. The Bell System had to be barred from engaging in improper conduct in the interchange and equipment markets.[27]

Judge Greene was correct in concluding that spinning off either Bell Labs or Western Electric would not address the anticompetitive behaviors that lurked in the Bell System's coordination of its local and long-distance markets. He was wrong in concluding that a lesser remedy—one addressed to particular contractual practices—could not meet the challenge. A major example of these practices were Bell's bogus technical objections to interconnection, which should be right up the FCC's alley. But Judge Greene's own decided view on the dismal performance of the FCC led him to adopt a more drastic remedy, which, ironically, increased the FCC's rate-setting duties, especially in connection with access charges between the BOCs and the long-distance carriers. Judge Greene, moreover, explicitly acknowledged that the FCC retained great discretion in setting these charges.[28] The point took on added irony because no one knew for sure which portions of the old integrated Bell System were subsidizing which others, or for what purposes. Yet Judge Greene never stopped to explain why he had such confidence in the FCC to deal with the complex regulatory matters he dumped into its lap when he was confident that it would fumble the far simpler question of determining which outside equipment was compatible with the Bell System. Nor did he discuss at this juncture the procompetitive decisions of the FCC. Only later, in discussing why the new AT&T should be free of restrictions on line-of-business decisions (except those related to data processing), did he observe that

> the regulatory decisions which introduced competition into the interexchange market are themselves relatively recent. It was not until 1978 that the provision of regular long distance telephone service became subject to competition. . . . The FCC decisions allowing interexchange carriers to expand their service offerings

by reselling and sharing AT&T services have likewise been in force only for the last several years.[29]

These new developments did not lead Judge Greene to reevaluate his prior negative judgment about the effectiveness of the FCC in bringing about competitive policies. He was dead set on working the change.

Implementation

The Bell System decree faced considerable logistical problems in parceling out assets across the various corporate entities. Nor, in light of the complex regulatory environment, could Judge Greene's decree expire once the mandated reorganization was completed. In addition, he introduced multiple provisions, each deceptively simple, that either prohibited or required certain kinds of behaviors from the new business entities (including the slimmed-down AT&T) created under the decree. All of these provisions were subject to Judge Greene's continuing oversight. Judge Greene was well aware that his initial opinion supplied only the first chapter of a looming chain novel. He kept his court open for business so that the Department of Justice (DOJ), AT&T, and the new BOCs could apply at any time "for such further orders or directions as may be necessary or appropriate for the construction or carrying out of this modification of Final Judgment, for the modification of any of the provisions hereof, for the enforcement of compliance herewith, and for the punishment of any violation hereof."[30] There is little doubt that Judge Greene inserted this provision to eliminate any possible objection that his future actions under the decree would have to satisfy the "grievous wrong" standard of *Swift & Co.* He prized continuity more than finality, and in several places wrote explicit directives to reconsider provisions in the decree.

In fairness, Judge Greene knew of the risks of his bold venture. He protested that he had "no wish to be engaged on a long-range basis in oversight" of his consent decree.[31] The telecommunications industry has a more rapid rate of technical innovation than meatpacking, music, and shoemaking. Undue delay in implementation would adversely affect the rate of innovation. But the die had already been cast when those soothing words appeared midway through a dense sixty-seven page opinion—written only one year after the initial decree, but *before* the reorganization was in place. Over the life of the decree, Judge Greene operated a de facto administrative agency to respond to a wide range of disputes. Unable to handle all those issues by himself, Judge Greene actively relied on the advice of the Justice Department before issuing his own decisions. I provide here a brief sampler.

The LATAs. The first major challenge before Judge Greene required him to divide the telecommunications market between local and long-distance carriers and to allocate the phone business within and across BOCs. Within a unified system, no one is troubled unduly about formal distinctions between local and long-distance calls. Basic economic and legal principles point toward allowing the single provider to use the cheapest technical method consistent with reliable service. But once the telecommunications world is divided into local exchanges with monopoly power and competitive long-distance carriers, the question of who gets what jobs is no longer a matter of efficiency alone; it is also a matter of turf and interconnection fees among unrelated entities.

In setting up the system for telephone calls that move across the different BOCs, the long-distance carrier gets the middle third of the call between the two local BOCs, even if it is tricky to set interconnection fees at both junction points. But it is much more difficult to allocate business within the multistate territories of each BOC. Leaving all intra-BOC phone calls local would cut out a large portion of the long-line business for AT&T and any new entrant. The alternative is to make virtually all calls within any BOC territory long-distance calls, so that local calls cover only those calls made within traditional and tiny local exchange areas. But that extreme solution creates efficiency losses by making just about any call a long-distance call, which then raises the question of whether they should be billed separately as such.

At the suggestion of the Bell System, Judge Greene split the difference by devising special areas for exclusive BOC use. These so-called Local Access and Transport Areas (LATAs) were larger than the traditional local exchange, and smaller than the BOC territories. From the outset, Judge Greene was alert to the parties' strategic interests. He rejected the tiny LATAs that were preferred by many independent telephone companies, who were *not* parties to the decree. Instead he opted for LATAs that would enable the BOCs to survive—some 160 of them, none larger than any single state, instead of the 7,000 or so local exchanges spread across the country. Though befitting an industrial planner more than a champion of competitive markets, Judge Greene's mid-size solution solved some real problems by reducing the number of contact points that a new long-distance carrier had to achieve. It also prevented the near-total disappearance of local phone calls from the system.

Yet the oddities of this compromise have to be noted as well. For starters, it made many phone calls within a BOC three-legged when a direct connection was technically easy to achieve. But the efficiency losses of this configuration could not be removed without sending the entire reorganization into a tailspin. At the same time, distinctions between local (toll-free) and long-distance (toll) calls were hopelessly muddled, but Judge Greene—ironically, given that he favored federal rule earlier in the process—held that *state* regulatory commissions had exclusive jurisdiction over that question.[32] Finally, LATAs effectively squelched the effort of new carriers to demand interconnection for the purpose of handling local calls. Part of the implicit price of the breakup was to *limit* competition at the local exchange level by denying new entrants interconnection rights.

While Judge Greene might in time have opened these markets to competition by forcing the BOCs to connect rival carriers, the decree precluded this approach. On the question of intra-LATA competition, Judge Greene acknowledged the jurisdictional limitations on the reach of his decree but hoped to rely on the same state commissions he had previously lambasted for their failure to open up those same markets, and held that his own limited role was to prevent obstructionism by the BOCs.[33] Throughout the elaborate quasi-administrative proceedings, Judge Greene failed to revisit the central challenge: Did his complex system lead to any kind of social improvement? In the midst of the regulatory morass, Judge Greene only spoke loudly in the abstract about benefits of competition to the American people.[34]

Judge Greene's LATA decision also revealed an incipient, if inevitable, clash between his jurisdiction and that of the FCC. The conflict was precipitated by the FCC's decision to approve rate increases for local subscribers to cover the needed interchange fees. Judge Greene took vocal exception to a regulatory decision he could not control, especially to its consequences "particularly among the black, the young, and the urban poor."[35] That complaint, though, showed an insufficient awareness of the tension in any ratemaking exercise. Any system that looks for allocative efficiency will tend to adopt high local charges because that segment of the market is relatively inelastic. But if redistribution is the goal, then the long-distance calls will bear this burden, where it will (given higher elasticity as of 1983) result in greater economic dislocation. Instead of facing this dilemma head on, Judge Greene returned to an inconclusive discussion of whether the long-lines were subsidized by the local calls or vice versa, which arose precisely because his 1982 consent decree contained no sensible findings on the cross-subsidy question.

This episode raises a serious debate over the relative strengths of regulation and antitrust for dealing with issues of market structure and firm practices. Huber, Kellogg, and Thorne have come down four-square on the side of antitrust law, on the grounds that it corrects past mistakes rather than seeking to work out matters in advance, while the market waits.[36] They are right in insisting that the ultimate choice must come to grips with the unhappy reality of relative imperfections: Both systems have glaring weaknesses, so that the "best" solution can only minimize the inevitable dislocations. But their analysis is subject to the critical caveat that the antitrust laws work well only so long as decrees remain linked in scope and limited in ambition. The Bell consent decree did not.

Electronic Publishing. In April 1989, Judge Greene granted AT&T's application to modify a provision of the decree that had prohibited the company from engaging in electronic publishing over its own transmission facilities. Because several other carriers had gained extensive capacity in this industry, Judge Greene no longer feared that AT&T occupied a "bottleneck" position. Without question, he reached the right result. But again, that decision did not undo the initial mistake of barring AT&T from the business back in 1982. Electronic publishing poses no risk that the regulated firm will use clever transfer-pricing devices to preclude rivals, all of whom could have switched to an independent carrier. Instead, the initial decree relied on the static assumption that the then current state of the market should be used to evaluate the potential for bottleneck abuse even in the face of free entry. The effect of this restriction was to keep one major competitor out of a market for seven years—which, while not a catastrophe, is hardly a blessing.

Lines-of-Business Restrictions. A modification question with far larger stakes arose shortly thereafter. Under the first of the "triennial reviews" that the Justice Department had "pledged" to supply, the BOC sought to modify the line-of-business restrictions that Judge Greene had imposed in the initial decree. Reliance on the Department of Justice reports showed just how much the consent decree apparatus had morphed into a closet administrative agency. (No ordinary lawsuit elicits routine comments from forty or so parties.) The review raised vexing procedural issues: Did the DOJ owe any deference to the findings of the district court? Did it make a difference that Judge Greene had special expertise in this particular area? Both questions having been answered in the negative, the inquiry turned to the consent decree itself, which provided that the line-of-business restriction "shall be removed upon a showing by the petitioning BOC that there is no substantial possibility that it could use its monopoly power to impede competition in the market it seeks to enter."[37]

The point of the initial business-entry prohibition was to prevent the cross-subsidy that could have taken place under the old, unified Bell System, which could use revenues from its monopoly operations to subsidize the competitive side of its business. But while that story works for possible entry into the interexchange operations (where high interconnection costs could prove ruinous to a BOC's rivals), it is doubtful that the BOCs could design switches to favor their local activities. Still, Judge Greene not only denied the BOCs' modification request with respect to interexchange; he also held that the BOCs did not meet their burden of proof for lifting the manufacturing restriction, on the grounds that the cross-subsidy risk would remain.[38] One wonders whether Bill Baxter would have agreed. Finally, with respect to information services, Judge Greene issued another remand to DOJ, holding (dubiously) that that question should be governed not by the rigid modification standards of the lines-of-business provision but by a more forgiving clause, dealing with modifications generally that did not impose an explicit burden of proof on the BOCs.[39] A "triennial" review, it appears, does not easily run its course. The central question of whether the risk of monopolization was offset by technological improvements remained largely hidden from view.

The AT&T/McCaw Merger. Shortly before the Bell consent decree was overtaken by the 1996 Telecom Act, Judge Greene was asked to modify the

1982 decree to permit AT&T's proposed purchase of the McCaw Cellular system. The issue arose because the decree prohibited AT&T from acquiring "the stock or assets of any BOC," and McCaw, through its aggressive acquisition program, held minority interests in cellular systems that the BOCs had taken over after divestiture. Holding that the modification of the consent decree was governed by the *Rufo* standard for modifying consent decrees rather than the strict demands of *Swift & Co.*, Judge Greene rightly found that the decree should be modified because the development and expansion of the cellular market had not been foreseen in 1982. Without a waiver of the anti-acquisition provision, the deal could not have received the usual public-interest analysis under the Tunney Act. But again: so long as Tunney Act review remains a requirement for all complex transactions, what advantage is there to a consent decree that adds another layer to an already laborious process? A less ambitious decree—one that only addressed the wrongs that prompted the finding of antitrust liability—would have constituted a simpler but more effective approach.

Why Less Is More

Judge Greene's many opinions reflect his intelligence and fortitude. But that is just what makes consent decrees such a treacherous business. If so able and energetic a judge gets many of the small questions right but still makes a mess of matters, the explanation must be structural. Ongoing oversight makes the consent decree look like the work of a permanent commission, without the staff or appropriations to support it. Its delays and confusions are similar to those in the FCC or the state commissions, but the dysfunctionality goes further. The Bell consent decree was wedded to a stagnant view of technology formed with the Bell System as of 1982. Systematic updates for a myriad of technical innovations are not in the cards. Rather, the challenges of implementation, such as forming LATAs, block a reexamination of the initial static assumptions. In time, advanced forms of integrated technology undercut the neat divisions between local and long-distance equipment that undergirded the original decree,[40] as well as those among different types of services. As often as not, however, the response was stubborn judicial insistence on the initial conditions. For example, Judge Greene had to be reined in by the District of Columbia Court of Appeals when, after denying a jury trial, he held NYNEX in contempt and fined it $1,000,000 for violating the decree by supplying information services instead of customer premises equipment—despite compelling expert testimony (from Peter Huber) on how the two overlapped.

In addition, the traditional administrative process, for all its lumbering incompetence, is not subject to the inherent limitation of binding only the parties to the litigation. Selective intervention cannot work when any industry-wide restructuring necessarily has to deal with nonparties and new parties as well, including all the non-Bell phone companies and the FCC. All matters of procedure and orders are complicated by this dual level of operation. For the FCC, the conflict is greater because its independent jurisdiction means that it can issue orders (especially to decree nonparties) that undercut some consent decree objectives. The situation cried out for a more modest solution. Given the right frame of mind, on balance the FCC could do a better job than Judge Greene if the only question were institutional competence. But no institutional choice could have saved the telecommunications industry from regulators that had a fundamentally wrongheaded view of their overall mission.

That point is demonstrated anew by the subsequent history of the 1996 Telecommunications Act, where the central mistake was to seek to mandate individual connections ordering the resale of unbundled network elements at bargain prices in order to jumpstart the same "competitive" solution that had necessarily eluded Judge Greene.[41] But there, too, the failure is traced to one simple point. If the distinctive feature of network industries is that they cannot facilitate voluntary interconnection agreements, then by all means order those connections on some omnibus solution and call it a day. If a distinctive feature of this industry is the need for cross subsidies, then impose equal tax on all competitors, not just some. Two simple principles. Following them could have avoided the loss of billions, both under the 1982 Bell System consent decree and thereafter.

4

Microsoft

Though young by antitrust standards, *United States v. Microsoft* is already the stuff of legends. The case rested on claims of misuse of market position by a firm that holds a dominant market position—that is, Microsoft's control of its computer operating system.

The simplest way to understand the government's case is to treat it like a common-carrier case. Stripped to their essentials, the traditional rules required such carriers to supply services to all comers on (1) reasonable and (2) nondiscriminatory terms. Both of these elements raise real questions. The "reasonableness" analysis starts from the premise that competitive prices cannot be set in network industries, so that state regulation, halting and imperfect as it is, must set rates high enough to allow the regulated firm to gain a reasonable return on its invested capital, but low enough to avoid the risk of monopoly profits. Fixing rates when the cost of service is not, or need not be, uniform across different customers is no easy task. The "nondiscrimination" requirement is intended to deal with the risk of diverse preferences among users of the system. The allocation of fixed costs of construction cannot be unique, and the fear is that the carrier will charge people different rates for identical services that can be supplied at equal cost.

The *Microsoft* case differs from this simple model in two ways. First, the question of pricing services is *not* part of the problem. The only question is reasonable and nondiscriminatory access to a system that occupies a dominant position. Once that challenge is settled against Microsoft by defining its server as a separate market segment, there is no institutional reason why the judicial system cannot answer the access question—even though it is manifestly incapable of setting, as opposed to reviewing, rates. So long as the firm has a dominant position, it has a duty of service. In this case, that translates into imposing interconnection obligations—much like in the railroad cases of the early twentieth century, when the same structural problem was handled through antitrust litigation, under a set of rules known as the "essential facilities doctrine."[1]

Second, an operating system works like a hub of a complex network that links writers of software applications with the end-users who desire their products. The model for understanding the basic arrangements is that of two-sided markets, whose central feature is that the demand on one side of the market is tied to the demand on the other.[2] For example, merchants will sign on to a credit card system only if they know that potential customers will use the cards, while the customers will sign on to the system only if they know that merchants will accept the cards. Two features of these markets bear note. First, it is not possible to use marginal cost-pricing for all parties. Rather, the common pattern is that the more favorable price terms will go to that side of the market which has the more variable response. The standard terms for payment cards have put the bulk of the costs on the merchants so that more resources can be spent on wooing consumers.[3] But the ostensible cross-subsidies redound to the merchants' indirect benefit by expanding the base of cardholders. Second, the number of independent networks is generally limited. Tiny networks are of little value to participants on either side, so that networks tend to merge or interconnect for efficiency reasons, which make it difficult to apply conventional antitrust rationales to their behavior.

The principles of two-sided markets apply to the computer industry. In the middle of the market stands the owner of the operating system. On one side are the customers who use the system; on the other, the designers of software applications. The larger the number of software applications, the more attractive the operating system is to end-users. The greater the number of end-users, the more attractive the operating system is to writers of software applications. The greater the success of the system, the more likely it is to receive support and upgrades over its life.[4] These powerful tendencies help explain why a dominant operating system is likely to maintain its position over time—or to suffer a catastrophic failure by mass migration to some newer and better system. They also explain why, for network industries, a single supplier offers an efficient outcome.[5] A forcible fragmentation of the market creates competition, but it also undercuts the positive network effects of a single operating system. At the same time, there is no role for price regulation to cover the cost of an operating system—which, when adjusted for quality improvements, continues to fall rapidly over time with technological improvements.

Keeping this simplified account of the liability issues in mind helps in understanding the central virtue of the Microsoft consent decrees. Those decrees represent a marked advance over the decrees issued in earlier cases. They tied the remedies closely to the underlying violations of antitrust law and, in particular, to the interconnection obligation that the common carrier model suggests. The Microsoft consent decrees resisted energetic attempts to impose major structural changes on Microsoft, or to limit the lines of businesses that it could enter; and they carefully limited their effective periods so that they did not become more of a burden than a benefit.

The 1994 Consent Decree

The first *Microsoft* decree arose out of a suit that the Antitrust Division filed against Microsoft in August 1993 and settled shortly thereafter in July 1994. The central complaint concerned Microsoft's contracting practices with respect to the sale of its operating systems to Original Equipment Manufacturers (OEMs). Some of those licenses required OEMs to pay a "per-processor" licensing fee for all units they shipped, whether or not these used Microsoft's operating system. This pattern of exclusive-dealing parallels the antitrust violations in the *ASCAP/BMI* cases. It also tracks United Shoe's exclusive licenses before they were struck down in 1918. In addition, Microsoft backed up its exclusive-dealing regime with negotiated minimum purchase amounts from OEMs. These minimums could roll over to future contracts, which further induced OEM manufacturers to shy away from competing systems.

As in the earlier cases, the question is whether the restrictive practices more than offset any efficiencies that the exclusive-dealing provision might generate, given that any OEM who wished to adopt a rival operating system had to pay twice for the privilege—once to Microsoft under its general obligation, and a second time to the rival operating system vendor. Herbert Hovenkamp has suggested that the answer is "yes," arguing that

> nothing in the IP laws authorizes or legitimizes per processor licensing practices. Indeed, the practice hinders rather than promotes innovation by suppressing the opportunities of smaller rivals who cannot realistically compete to have their operating systems installed on new computers.[6]

His point is that, due to the exclusive practice, smaller rivals who cannot enter all segments of the market are effectively precluded from entering any segment at all. That is true, but it does not exhaust the analysis. Unlike price-fixing agreements that lack any efficiency justification, the exclusive-dealing provision does have positive efficiency consequences of the sort protected under intellectual property law. Microsoft's monopoly position over its operating system works just like a patentee's exclusive rights over its covered invention. (There was no allegation that Microsoft obtained the dominant position for its operating system through illegal activity.)[7]

At this juncture, antitrust law has to identify a trade-off that is familiar in the patent area: Is the negative impact of the exclusion greater than the positive impulse that exclusive rights give to early inventions? In focusing solely on the activities of the new entrant, Hovenkamp fails to take into account the social benefits from the more rapid development of the underlying operating system. To be sure, if the exclusive-dealing provisions are valid, they are valid indefinitely and not just for a limited term, as with patents. But then the period of effective dominance of any operating system is uncertain given the possibility of technological circumvention—which has proved so instrumental, for example, in undermining the BOCs' once-formidable last-mile monopoly after the displacement of the consent decree by cellular systems, cable, Internet, and electrical portals into the home. While the exclusive effects may in the end matter more than the spur to early invention, one should at least ask the question.

Microsoft's exclusive licenses, moreover, had features that are consistent with general principles of marginal cost-pricing. The first unit of any operating system is expensive to produce. Subsequent copies are relatively cheap. The use of quantity discounts thus has the advantage of imposing a zero marginal price on the purchaser of the operating system, at least over a certain range of purchases. Rolling over the unused licenses to later years is yet another way to allow the buyer to obtain additional units at close to zero marginal cost. No doubt the pricing strategies are a real impediment to outsiders. As in *United Shoe*, though, the correlation between the claims of competitors and those of consumers is imperfect. Anticompetitive effects come in a bundle with efficiency considerations.

Another point of uncertainty is the impact of exclusive license provisions on the dominance of Microsoft's operating system. That issue, as already discussed, arose in both the *ASCAP/BMI* and *United Shoe* litigation, and in both settings eliminating the offending contract terms had little effect. In the server setting, too, many OEMs might well prefer to stick with a single operating system for all their units even if not required to do so. Single suppliers reduce the complexities of managing supply chains and of dealing with customers, tasks that involve substantial expenses. Banning exclusive-dealing provisions might *harm* consumers by making it impossible for them to pay a lower price for an exclusive-dealing arrangement than they do for a contract that allows them to do business elsewhere. These cross-currents make it difficult to infer here, any more than in *ASCAP/BMI* or *United Shoe*, that removing the offending provision from the contracts would likely have a large impact on the shape of the market.

In negotiating these cross-currents, the 1994 draft consent decree did not make the mistake of imposing large structural remedies in response to particular contract practices. The prohibitions in the consent decree honed in on the practices that had been identified as anticompetitive, chiefly those which tended to create exclusive rights.

Licensing. The draft decree barred per-processor licenses, lump-sum licenses (which could act as a substitute for per-processor fees), and long-term licenses (more than one year). The effort was to stop the lock-in effect of the exclusive licenses and the double payments they required. The one oddity—closely resembling the *United Shoe* case—was the insistence that Microsoft could *not* offer at lower prices exclusive licenses for greater than one year, even to a willing buyer. In similar fashion, renewals, which were without penalty and at "the sole discretion" of the OEM, could not be made for more than a single year, either. And, most notably, there was an anti-tie-in provision, beyond the scope of the original complaint:

> (E) Microsoft shall not enter into any License Agreement in which the terms of that agreement are expressly or impliedly conditioned upon:
> (1) the licensing of any other Covered Product, Operating System Software product or other product (provided, however, that this provision in and of itself shall not be construed to prohibit Microsoft from developing integrated products).

Intended to prevent the leverage of one dominant product into another market, this provision would come to loom large in subsequent litigation.

Nondisclosure Agreements. The *Microsoft* litigation involved a charge that Microsoft had "imposed nondisclosure agreements on some ISVs [Independent Software Vendors] which would restrict their ability to work for competing operating systems companies and to develop competing products for an unreasonably long period of time."[8] The consent decree contained two remedial provisions. First, nondisclosure agreements (NDAs) may be imposed for limited periods of time during the development phase of the process, but not for a period longer than one year. Second, recipients of this confidential information may not use it in dealing with products for a competitive operating system. The purpose of this provision was to ensure that a company could work on software products not only for Microsoft but for its competitors—*without* using Microsoft trade secrets to aid in its work on competitive systems. That result requires that Microsoft licensees accept internal safeguards to avoid the cross-pollination of ideas. In practice, this portion of the 1994 consent decree represents a neat effort to reconcile anticompetitive concerns over exclusive-development agreements with the legitimate claim of proprietary protection for trade secrets. While the revised NDAs counter anticompetitive behavior, they also create a risk that Microsoft's trade secrets will be misappropriated notwithstanding the NDA. But the balance is defensible.

The DOJ and Microsoft had reached a quick agreement on the substantive terms of the consent decree. What remained was to gain the approval of

U.S. District Judge Stanley Sporkin. Sporkin, however, took a very expansive view of his role under the Tunney Act, treated its public interest requirement as though it authorized a comprehensive review of the merits of the underlying settlement, and concluded that the proposed decree did not address adequately the full range of anticompetitive practices.[9] His manifest hostility was evident in his initial procedural decision, which allowed the law firm of Wilson Sonsini to file a brief in opposition to the consent decree without identifying the parties on whose behalf the brief had been written. His decision rested on the need to avoid retaliation against those parties from Microsoft. But by granting the motion, Sporkin in effect vouched for the credibility of the charges, without taking any direct evidence on the point.

Next, Sporkin asked the DOJ to provide detailed records of its internal investigation, including its evaluation of each of Microsoft's contractual provisions or business practices, to be supplemented with accounts of what issues were discussed or kept off the table in the settlement negotiation.[10] Sporkin then pressed the DOJ to follow up on charges made in the Wilson Sonsini memo, based on the book *Hard Drive*,[11] that Microsoft had engaged in the practice of announcing new software releases early, sometimes called "vaporware," in order to freeze consumers from buying other products.[12] Finally, Judge Sporkin thought that the parties' proposed remedies were insufficient to "pry open" Microsoft to competition. Throughout, he relied heavily on the expansive view that Judge Greene had taken of his Tunney Act powers in the Bell System case.[13]

On appeal, a panel of the U.S. Court of Appeals for the District of Columbia reversed the decision below and unanimously approved the proposed consent decree. Judge Laurence Silberman's opinion read the Tunney Act to preclude the wide discretion that Judge Sporkin had claimed for himself. Instead, the appeals court followed the dominant precedent that the statute was not intended to eliminate all prosecutorial discretion in negotiating consent decrees. The court's tolerance for Sporkin's independent judicial initiatives was far lower than that accorded to Judge Greene, whose crucial 1982 breakup order had received no appellate review, except for the one-sentence affirmation in the Supreme Court. Symptomatic of the shift in attitude, Judge Silberman quoted at length from Justice Rehnquist's dissent to the Supreme Court's pro forma affirmance of the Bell System breakup, on the separation of power issues.[14] In addition, Judge Silberman relied on the D.C.

Circuit Court decision in the triennial review cases, which later clipped Judge Greene's wings under the Tunney Act. The operative test was whether the consent decree was "within the *reaches* of the public interest," even if it was not necessarily "the one that will *best* serve society."[15] The appeals court not only ordered Judge Sporkin to enter the proposed consent order, in a short *per curiam* opinion appended to the substantive disposition; it also removed Judge Sporkin from the case on the grounds that he had deviated so far from acceptable standards of behavior in this case—by pushing so hard on secret filings and extrajudicial evidence—that his conduct showed an "actual bias" that required dismissal from the case.

The one major substantive battle over the 1994 decree came three years later on the question of what counted as an "integrated product." The pertinent tie-in provision, quoted earlier, differs from the limits on contractual provisions in that limitations on design features are more intrusive into the core business of the regulated firm. While all section 2 Sherman Act cases require a balance between the anticompetitive practices that the decree bars and the efficiency losses that the decree simultaneously imposes, the presumption ought in most cases shift against imposing design restrictions, in light of their higher efficiency cost. The same consideration counsels a cautious reading of design restrictions that do make it into a consent decree.

The question came to a head when Microsoft sought to launch a new operating system tied to the latest version of its browser, Internet Explorer 4. Microsoft had previously required OEMs to install IE 4's precursor, IE 3, as part of Windows.[16] But they were not required to install IE 4, which was distributed to OEMs on a separate CD. Under the OEMs' licenses for Windows, however, that grace period ended in February 1998, and Microsoft now required OEMs to install Windows with IE 4. The DOJ sought to hold Microsoft in civil contempt and to get a preliminary injunction against the distribution of the new product—in the high-paced tech world, no small matter. In December 1997, District Judge Thomas Penfield Jackson denied the civil contempt motion on the ground that there was no clear and convincing evidence that the new launch violated the consent decree. But he granted the preliminary injunction, perceiving a substantial likelihood that the anti-tying provision had been violated.

The tying arrangement comes within the purview given that IE counts as an "other" covered product. The sole question is whether it is also shielded by the proviso that governs integrated products. The district court spent more time worrying about the requirements to prove illegal tie-in arrangements under the antitrust laws than on the particular exception incorporated into the decree. Thus it noted that illegal tie-ins tend to occur with respect to two products that are regarded as distinct by customers in the ordinary market, and which can be distributed as such. That was certainly the case with the new Windows operating system and IE 4. The key question, however, was not how the law of tie-ins might treat this particular provision but how it played out under the consent decree, which adopted a separate rule for "integrated products."

The definition section of the 1994 consent decree covered fourteen terms whose common meanings were already well established (for example, NDA and OEM). But the phrase "integrated product" was not among them. That phrase had been used, however, in earlier judicial decisions— for example, cases arising over IBM computer hardware that combined several distinct functions (such as external hard drives and memory) that in earlier times had been sold as separate products.[17] The integration made one product out of what had once been two, so it was not at all clear that tie-in law, which requires two separate products, applied. The district court in the IBM matter had indicated its willingness to make sure the defendant did not escape liability

> by pretending that two separate and distinct products are one. . . . However, where a court is dealing with what is physically and in fact a single product, Section 3 (of the Clayton Act) does not contemplate judicial dissection of that product into parts and the reconstitution of these parts into a tying agreement.[18]

The IBM cases also used the term "integration," which provided some guidance to interpret it in connection with the Microsoft consent decree: "Technological progress in component miniaturization has made possible the integration of additional memory and control functions and such additional integration has made possible cost reductions and enhanced utility."[19]

These decisions suggest the proper reading of the Microsoft consent decree, always remembering that it must be read first as a contract, not as an embodiment of Sherman Act tie-in jurisprudence.[20] Microsoft argued that any decision to sell two products together, either in the same box or on the same disk, falls within the scope of the proviso. That position, though, seems wrong both under the IBM precedents and in substance: It swallows the basic rule.[21] Yet, by the same token, it would be most unwise to conduct an investigation of all Microsoft's design decisions to decide whether the latest version of IE should have been hidden or disabled when sold by the OEM so that if the OEM decided to remove the IE icon from its desktop, it would become available to consumers only in a downloadable form. That inquiry would compel the court to determine whether a decision to expand the operating system was made opportunistically, more to exclude competitors than to benefit consumers. Answering that question requires the kind of second-guessing on technical issues that tends to give many Sherman Act section 2 cases a black eye.

The Jackson opinion never asked about the design gains from this configuration. Instead, in ways that hinted of the theory of the government's second Microsoft prosecution, Jackson stressed how the delivery of the single package could prevent browsers from becoming an alternative platform that could threaten the Windows monopoly. But here, too, that fear raises a set of antitrust issues outside the initial complaint, and gives no understanding of the proper meaning of "integrated product."

Judge Jackson's decision did not survive on appeal. In *Microsoft II*, Judge Stephen F. Williams first noted that the debate over the integrated products proviso arose over earlier versions of IE, so that it would be odd to conclude that the provision did not reach the very situation it was intended to cover. Second, Judge Williams concluded that so long as Microsoft could point to some efficiency gains from its integrated design, he would not use fine scales to weigh the relative strengths of the efficiency versus anticompetitive effects.[22] He cut through the murk:

> We think it quite possible . . . to find a construction of [the integrated product provision] that is consistent with the antitrust laws and accomplishes the parties' evident desires on entering the decree. The Department and [the European Director General—Competition] were concerned with the alleged anticompetitive effects of tie-ins. Microsoft's goal was to preserve its freedom to design products that consumers would like.

Antitrust scholars have long recognized the undesirability of having courts oversee product design, and any dampening of technological innovation would be at cross-purposes with antitrust law. Thus, a simple way to harmonize the parties' desires is to read the integration proviso . . . as permitting any genuine technological integration, regardless of whether elements of the integrated package are marketed separately.

This reading requires us, of course, to give substantive content to the concept of integration. We think that an "integrated product" is most reasonably understood as a product that combines functionalities (which may also be marketed separately and operated together) in a way that offers advantages unavailable if the functionalities are bought separately and combined by the purchaser.[23]

Microsoft III

Before these issues were fully sorted out, the government launched its second antitrust suit against Microsoft in May 1998. Under both sections 1 and 2 of the Sherman Act, the government challenged a range of contractual provisions and business practices that Microsoft had used to promote its Internet Explorer. (Microsoft's business objective was to catch and displace the then dominant Netscape web browser, which had made its successful debut in 1994 as an application that could run on a variety of operating systems.) Twenty states and the District of Columbia through their attorneys general also filed antitrust actions, covering much the same ground.[24] The combined cases again came before Judge Jackson, who, after an extensive trial, found against Microsoft on several theories.[25] Shortly thereafter, without conducting a separate evidentiary hearing, Judge Jackson ordered the breakup of Microsoft into two separate units, one for its Windows operating system and the other for the remaining parts of its business.[26]

In a unanimous *per curiam* decision, the appellate court reversed in part on the liability, and entirely on the breakup remedy.[27] Judge Jackson was removed from the case, retroactively, for his work in the remedial phase of the case because of improper contacts with the press and the public, and, prospectively, from dealing with the case on remand. The suit was assigned to Judge Colleen Kollar-Kotelly, who, on rehearing, entered a far more modest consent decree that focused on Microsoft's specific anticompetitive practices. That consent decree, accepted by both the United States and Microsoft, was in turn challenged by several states, whose insistence on more stringent remedies was rebuffed first before Judge Kollar-Kotelly and, when Massachusetts alone carried on, in the Court of Appeals for the District of Columbia. As with the previous consent decrees, the critical issues in *Microsoft III* revolved around how the underlying theory of antitrust liability guides the choice of antitrust remedies, given the risks of under- and overinclusion. On this point, overinclusion was the greater risk, given the tendency for technological innovation to undermine market dominance.

The government's claims in *Microsoft III* covered a broad range of unilateral practices, including various forms of predation, exclusion, and tie-in arrangements, only some of which had been addressed in *Microsoft I*. The first group of charges centered on the issue of monopoly maintenance, which requires proof of a monopoly or dominant position in the market *and* unilateral practices that improperly exploit that position for anticompetitive purposes. In dealing with the first prong, both the district and the circuit courts held that the relevant market was that for Intel-compatible PC operating systems, which excluded both Unix and Mac systems.[28] That decision rested on the conclusion that Microsoft enjoyed some degree of price control in the PC market because of the cost consumers would pay for the shift to Mac or Unix, which did not in any event provide the same set of features (for instance, fewer applications). Sound as that conclusion is as a first approximation, it misses the dynamic element of competition, which Microsoft stressed in reply.

Even though it is a network industry, Microsoft faces the risk of an erosion of its dominant position. Apple installed Intel chips and parlayed its success with the iPod into a larger market share. Linux became more accessible to a sophisticated group of consumers. In addition, some new operating system or other, as yet unknown, innovation might come along and induce mass migration from Windows. Uneasy lies the head that wears the crown: Microsoft has to fear that its products will be "commoditized," rendering a unique and dominant product no more distinctive than a brand of toothpaste. To some minds, Netscape posed that risk.

Such threats limit Microsoft's short-term use of monopoly power. They may induce Microsoft to act more cautiously on pricing issues and to innovate more aggressively than if it has a guaranteed future market. The narrow market definition should not be allowed at the remedial stage to obscure the broader market forces that have operated on Microsoft from the outset and continue to do so today, when the company still runs the risk that a resourceful Google or other unknown competitor can place its own platform atop the Microsoft operating system.

The more controversial part of the government's case in *Microsoft III* concerned the catalogue of illegal practices that Microsoft was found to have deployed to maintain its monopoly position. Microsoft's advantage was that software writers preferred to write for systems with large consumer bases, while consumers, in turn, preferred to buy operating systems for which many applications were written. This network effect was a replication of the same issue as *Microsoft I*, but Microsoft now faced a serious challenge to its dominant position by the arrival of "middleware," in the form of the Netscape browser coupled with the Java "write once, run anywhere" potential. Middleware has its own distinctive set of specifications for interconnection, which rely on a set of Application Programming Interfaces, or APIs. APIs are essential to allow the interconnectivity and, hence, interoperability of computer programs. For example, they allow Windows to make thousands of different kinds of computers run the same set of software applications, typically prepared by non-Microsoft vendors.[29] That task is obviously critical owing to the industry's network basis. Microsoft, for example, had to make its APIs available to software developers so as to ensure compatibility between systems.

In *Microsoft III*, the government stressed the commoditization theme: Netscape could sit on top of Windows, so that software developers could write their applications for it instead of Windows. But the doomsday scenario for Microsoft was that "developers might begin to rely upon APIs exposed by the middleware for basic routines rather than relying upon the API set included in Windows."[30] Netscape could then connect to multiple operating systems by interconnecting itself to any one of a number of new operating systems at the bottom layer. The introduction of the new middle layer thus held the potential to undercut the dominant position of Windows in the operating market. Shortly after its 1994 introduction,

Netscape had taken the position of the dominant browser, and thus was widely viewed as an obvious candidate to subvert Windows. But the possibility remains so long as *any* new entrant into the browser market is able to adopt the strategy that was then open to Netscape. The bottom line was, therefore, that the new browsers, or some other platform innovation, could allow competition to take place both at the level of middleware and of the operating system.

Motive established, the government described the tactics, legal and illegal, that Microsoft had adopted to meet the Netscape threat. Obviously, Microsoft developed IE to establish its own presence in the web browser space. But no one thought then, or thinks now, that antitrust law requires a firm like Microsoft, with a dominant position in one segment of the market, not to compete at all in any adjacent sector. The price to consumer welfare from such blanket prohibitions on competitive responses is just too high, and certainly Netscape is no more entitled to a legally protected monopoly in the browser space than Microsoft is for Windows. Simple product excellence would count as a form of "competition on the merits," as it is sometimes called.[31] Ultimately, therefore, the government's case against Microsoft depended on isolating particular practices, including the integration of the IE browser into the Windows operating system, that posed grief to competitors without supplying offsetting advantages to consumers. Once the government had identified some anticompetitive practice, it would then be up to Microsoft to justify that practice on efficiency grounds.

In evaluating the government's claims, note that even the use of a zero price makes perfectly good sense if the marginal cost of the additional copy is zero and its dissemination has indirect benefits to the supplier. Yet at the same time, the pricing considerations are of little or no relevance if the substantive terms of the contract are found to have restrictive effects. The difficult cases are the mixed situations in which a practice is both defensible on efficiency grounds and vulnerable to attack as a restrictive practice.

The first group of charged offenses revolved around the restrictions that Microsoft placed on OEMs to protect its dominant position. Both the district court and the court of appeals rightly found that Microsoft engaged in anticompetitive practices when its licenses included provisions against "(1) removing any desktop icons, folders, or 'Start' menu entries; (2) altering the initial boot sequence; and (3) otherwise altering the appearance of the Windows."[32] The first practice made it more difficult for OEMs to "prein-stall" a rival browser on the computer, both because of capacity constraints and the confusion that multiple browsers allegedly sowed in consumers (in turn placing heavier demands on an OEM's customer service operations). The restriction on the boot-up sequence made it more difficult for an OEM to promote another browser (such as Netscape) that might have greater consumer appeal. While the effect of this restriction was limited (once the power was turned on, the OEM could ask users if they preferred to choose some other browser), it had no efficiency justification. Microsoft's argument that it was entitled to copyright protection for its appearance elements rightly fell on deaf ears.[33] Finally, the restriction on changes in the desktop appearance was declared unlawful because it makes it difficult to promote rival browsers.

All three conclusions fall well within the parameters of conventional antitrust law. Each wrong points to its own precise remedy: Ban the identi-fied practice. If the *United Shoe* history is any guide, there is no reason to expect that the prohibitions, even when fully enforced, would have much effect on overall business patterns in light of the efficiency advantages to OEMs of dealing with a single supplier. But each OEM would be free to deal only with Microsoft or with one or more alternative suppliers.

The second cluster of charges addressed the *technical* steps that Micro-soft had taken to bind IE to Windows. These were "excluding IE from the 'Add/Remove Programs' utility; designing Windows so as in certain cir-cumstances to override the user's choice of a default browser other than IE; and commingling code related to browsing and other code in the same files, so that any attempt to delete the files containing IE would, at the same time, cripple the operating system."[34]

As noted, an effort to base antitrust liability on design choices has the potential to cut deeply into ordinary (and efficient) practices. The court of appeals started from the proposition, already adopted in the *IBM* inte-grated products cases, that "courts are properly very skeptical about claims that competition has been harmed by a dominant firm's product design changes."[35] That deferential posture shaped the court's decision on Microsoft's design decision to override a user's choice of a default browser. While that feature squarely fits the definition of an anticompetitive practice under section 2, Microsoft persuaded the court of appeals that it had adopted it for valid technical reasons. Judicial deference rightly ended on the question of the add/remove feature: If that feature was in earlier versions of the operating system, no design imperative required it to be eliminated. And so long as Windows sits on the desktop, it is less likely that OEMs will install another system—unless, of course, they were compensated for it by rival vendors.

The last design issue, dealing with commingled code, is more difficult to answer. The restrictive element arises because no one can delete IE without deleting part of Windows. But the tighter integration could easily have led to higher technical innovation. In light of the conflicting evidence, the court of appeals upheld the finding of illegality below on the grounds that it was not "clearly erroneous." All three determinations are about right within a section 2 framework. As with the licensing practices, the precise specification of the wrong in the first and third cases leads to a specific remedy, which, if properly drafted, should stop any effort to use more expansive means to achieve the same strategic end.

A third set of charges concerned Microsoft's distribution agreements with Internet Access Providers (IAPs), defined to include Internet Service Providers (ISPs) and Online Services (OLS), like AOL. The gist of this charge was that "Microsoft extended valuable promotional treatment to the ten most important IAPs in exchange for their commitment to promote and distribute [IE] and to exile Navigator from the desktop."[36] Microsoft also offered ISPs special IE Access Kits that allowed for a personalization of their web sites. Judge Jackson characterized these practices as unlawful predation.

In what seems like a stunningly easy decision, the court of appeals reversed, for the simple reason that lower prices and better services are pro-competitive even when supplied by a dominant firm. But it drew the line at a provision in the agreement with AOL (and those with a handful of other IAPs) that stipulated that "AOL does not promote any non-Microsoft browser, nor provide software using any non-Microsoft browser except at the customer's request, and even then AOL will not supply more than 15% of its subscribers with a browser other than IE."[37] Both the district and appellate courts found that Netscape suffered a significant level of "foreclosure" from the use of this agreement, especially since the IAPs acted as the second major distribution channel for Netscape.

During the initial burst of web activity in 1997–98, Microsoft had also entered into a number of "first wave" exclusive dealing-agreements with Independent Software Vendors (ISVs). Both courts took a dim view of provisions that sought to make IE the default browser for linking local computers to so-called hypertext-based user interfaces. Assume that these liability judgments are sound, and once again the remedy follows from the violation: Exclude the use of this type of clause by the dominant player.

The same conclusion attaches to the determination that Microsoft had used its business muscle to persuade Apple and Intel to align themselves with IE against Sun and Netscape products. For antitrust purposes, the effectiveness of these threats is less important than their occurrence. Given its dominant position, an explicit or implicit threat not to support Apple or Intel products unless IE is installed in their systems counts as a refusal to deal that is allowable to competitive but not dominant firms (with, of course, some efficiency loss).[38] There was a further discussion of Microsoft's extended efforts to persuade these ISVs to enter into exclusive agreements that led them to use Microsoft's Java Virtual Machine (JVM), instead of Sun's or Netscape's JVMs, for software development. The court of appeals held that Microsoft's exclusive promotion agreements and its deception—making it appear that programs written for its JVM had "cross-platform" use when in fact they could only be used with Windows—also counted as anticompetitive practices in the absence of a credible justification.

Two other facets of *Microsoft III* round out the picture. First, the distribution of IE through OEMs and IAPs reduced the effectiveness of only two of the three major paths that Netscape had to get its products to market. The third path—downloading from the Internet—was one that Microsoft was powerless to block. In just one year (1998) computer users downloaded about 160 million copies of Netscape. New upgrades of both browsers came out relatively frequently (Microsoft had four major versions between August 1995 and October 1997), so that new downloads were likely to be common no matter which browser had been preinstalled on the original machine.

This observation does not detract from a finding of antitrust liability for constricting the two preferred channels of distribution, but it does explain why Microsoft could drive neither Netscape nor any other browser from the marketplace. Because the counterstrategies are cheap, they would have kicked in if Microsoft had sought to stiffen the terms on which IE was made available, just as a sharp increase in the cost of its operating system would have increased migration to Apple and Unix. Indeed, if some combination of Netscape and Java could have displaced Microsoft Windows in the short run, the downloading option would have proved only more valuable. Stated otherwise, even though Microsoft's exclusive practices surely had some effect on the overall structure of the market, the extent of that influence is surely open to doubt. There is an important lesson here. The proof of *causation* in antitrust cases does not follow simply from an identification of some illegal exclusive practice. Thousands of business decisions about the configuration of both Netscape and IE mattered to the relative shares of both products in the marketplace.

In the end, the court of appeals dismissed a claim of "attempted monopolization" (as opposed to monopoly maintenance), largely because the DOJ had not established the influence of Microsoft's practices in the browser "market" to the court's satisfaction. In dismissing this claim, the court of appeals also removed one of the liability props under the district court's proposed breakup. To the extent that the division of Microsoft was not tied to any particular theory of liability, the rejection of one theory of liability cast doubt on whether the district court could have, or should have, ordered the breakup for a more limited class of antitrust wrongs.

The second area of disputation involved the government's claim that it was illegal to bundle IE to the Microsoft operating system, when these could be sold separately. If Microsoft could distribute IE only separately, it would lose its running start over rival browsers. Yet that decision would deprive consumers who preferred IE of the advantages of a preinstalled system whose built-in connections might well enhance its overall performance. This debate, of course, hearkened back to the 1998 interpretive dispute about "integrated products" under the first consent decree in *Microsoft II*. The dispute now turned not on the language of the consent decree but on antitrust law itself; little, however, ultimately hung on the distinction. The court of appeals declined to view all ties per se illegal and opted for a rule of reason (which has greater appeal in cases where the two products are joined together physically instead of simply being sold together). After a long and inconclusive discussion, the appellate court remanded the tie-in claim for further consideration.[39]

The Aborted Breakup

The breakup is at the end of a list of remedial possibilities that includes both damages and injunctions. The two types of damage remedies are *tort* damages, which measure the losses suffered by others as a result of the illegal act, and *restitution* damages that are meant to disgorge from a defendant any gains or benefits it receives from its illegal practices. In addition, antitrust law contemplates the use of injunctive relief that prohibits practices that have been found illegal. Breakups count as a remedy of last resort. In dealing with the relationship between damages (tort and restitution) and injunctions, a central concern is whether any form of injunctive relief can provide adequate protection for parties injured by exclusive practices. The obvious rejoinder is that damages must be added into the mix, with respect to past losses. However, class actions or individual lawsuits are likely to founder on the question of antitrust causation.

An injunction can be narrowly tailored to specific practices. The danger of overbreadth is effectively met by properly drafting the terms of the injunction. Unfortunately, that technique is *not* available for setting damages, whether we focus on harm to society or benefits to Microsoft. There are no shortcuts to finding out the likely differences in the positions of all parties if Microsoft had taken only those procompetitive steps open to it under antitrust law.[40] One hypothetical damage inquiry, which looks to disgorging illegal gains, asks how Microsoft's optimal strategy would have influenced its revenue, profitability, and market share and those of its rivals, many of whom were not even on the scene. As a matter of sound procedure, Microsoft should be able to introduce explanations for its continued dominance of the browser market, including its zero price for IE and its multiple technical improvements, such as the modularized version of IE, which made it easier to interact with other applications.

As Kevin M. Murphy pointed out in his expert testimony for Microsoft, Netscape's market share would have declined about 25 percent among subscribers to all ISPs, whether or not IE was distributed under terms that met the standards of antitrust illegality.[41] The illegal terms did not appear to have a separate negative impact on Netscape's market share. Likewise, Murphy marshaled evidence that Netscape had not provided a consistent platform for Java that would have allowed it to support the same broad range of applications that ran on the Microsoft platform.[42] A showing of antitrust harm by a preponderance of evidence standard looked like an uphill battle. The injunction against specific contract terms did not require that proof.[43] Removing the anticompetitive practices makes it possible to attribute the resulting patterns of success and failure solely to competitive forces.

The possibility of significant underdeterrence still remains. In principle, that gap could be remedied by levying a fine calibrated to the aggregate measure of the social losses. That approach abandons any effort to assign those losses to any individual customer, but it does not answer the basic challenge. Setting fines also depends on resolving the very causation questions on which Murphy's evidence cast such doubt: Where are the aggregate losses, given the power of Microsoft's legal and effective strategies? The government's case flounders not because it is unable to figure out *which* competitors or consumers have been hurt but because it cannot show that *any*, or at least many, consumers have been hurt. In the limit, if Microsoft's anticompetitive practices had no effect on its market share or prices, then fines and tort recoveries should be set at zero as well.

Another way to finesse these difficulties is to take back any benefits that Microsoft may have received from its illegal practices. Unfortunately, that won't work, either. The benefits-received figure is hard to pin down for the same reason that it is difficult to measure the social losses: The lion's share of Microsoft's gains are attributable to its legal counterstrategies, and profits from illegal practices are hard to isolate. A court could set a fine for Microsoft equal to some fraction of its gross receipts, but in the absence of reliable evidence on causation, a judicial fine is also a bad proxy for either the private or social harm stemming (solely) from Microsoft's anticompetitive practices.

One can think of the Microsoft saga as an object lesson on the difficulties in any generalized tort theory of joint causation. In ordinary physical injury cases, joint causation questions are relatively rare because one person is not often shot or hit simultaneously by two individuals acting independently. In certain cumulative trauma cases (such as asbestos or toxic torts), joint causation questions are much more acute because of the presence of both (1) natural sources of pollution (analogous to Microsoft's legal responses—that is, no liability) and (2) the discharge of one or more of the defendants. The liability determination in *Microsoft* is analogous. One group of causes comprises the illegal conduct isolated and identified in *Microsoft I* and *Microsoft III*. The second group of causes implicates the legal, competitive responses that are allowed even to a dominant player under current law. An effort to estimate the relative contribution of these two causal classes requires a full inventory of the contribution of both classes, where the former are likely to dominate. In all likelihood, *no* fine is the best approximation of the correct result: The prior low estimate of aggregate damages implies that the danger of overdeterrence is far greater than that of underdeterrence. It is for good reason that neither court in *Microsoft III* introduced any form of damages into its calculation.

Any supposed shortcoming at this front, however, pales beside the massive overdeterrence and social dislocation that would have occurred had the appellate court affirmed Judge Jackson's order to break up Microsoft into two corporations. Ironically, that draconian remedy would have done nothing to rectify past losses to competitors or to undo illicit gains to Microsoft. But it would have had enormous negative consequences for future innovation in the computer industry (which for these purposes has to be broadly defined) by needlessly crippling one of its great players, in ways that would have had far more anticompetitive impact than any illegal practice of Microsoft. Before heading in that direction, it would have been wise for Judge Jackson to heed the lessons of the United Shoe and Bell System breakups, and of the history of antitrust consent decrees and judgments more generally. Two lessons leap out.

First, never break up integrated firms because their continued integrated operations generate substantial efficiency gains. This is surely the case for a firm like Microsoft, which grew internally and not through acquisitions. There is no merger or acquisition to be undone, and, owing to its organic growth, Microsoft has no obvious divisions that can be first isolated and then spun off pursuant to court order.

Second, never order a breakup that fails to deal with the monopoly power that generated the initial lawsuit. The failure to observe that constraint led to endless mischief when the Bell System was broken up into local operating companies, whose own operations were then hamstrung in order to counteract the BOCs' territorial monopolies. Judge Jackson's

ill-conceived breakup order, had it been executed, would have had similar
baleful effects. Supposed difficulties stemming from Microsoft's control of
Windows would remain untouched so long as Windows remained the
exclusive property of one of the two spun-off companies. As Herbert
Hovenkamp has written, "If the source of monopoly is the operating system, then the breakup does nothing to destroy the monopoly."[44] At the very
least, the spun-off firm could have exploited its position through price
increases. Indeed, it could easily and again face the glare of the antitrust law
for its unilateral practices, which would still be undertaken from a dominant position. Yet at the same time, the breakup would doubtless have generated huge transaction costs, operational delays and inefficiencies, and
contractual disputes in trying to assign assets, employees, and outside contracts to the two firms. The dislocations that accompanied the breakup of
the Bell System would have occurred here, too.

Judge Jackson entered his breakup order without comparing the
pluses and minuses with more tailored remedies. His brief inquiry never
touched on why Microsoft's antitrust violations caused social losses, and he
never asked a question that is critical in all monopolization cases: Was the
maintenance of the Microsoft monopoly a terrible vice or only an imper-
fection in a complicated world? It was therefore a simple matter for the
appellate court to conclude in *Microsoft III* that Judge Jackson's decree did
not stack up well against the remedial objectives:

> The District Court has not explained how its remedies decree
> would accomplish those objectives. Indeed, the court devoted a
> mere four paragraphs of its order to explaining its reasons for
> the remedy. They are: (1) Microsoft "does not yet concede that
> any of its business practices violated the Sherman Act"; (2) Micro-
> soft "continues to do business as it has in the past"; (3) Microsoft
> "has proved untrustworthy in the past"; and (4) the Govern-
> ment, whose officials "are by reason of office obliged and
> expected to consider—and to act in—the public interest," won
> the case, "and for that reason alone have some entitlement to a
> remedy of their choice." *Final Judgment*, at 62–63. Nowhere did
> the District Court discuss the objectives the Supreme Court
> deems relevant.[45]

The Kollar-Kotelly 2002 Final Judgment

Microsoft took a very different turn on remand, which graphically shows why, in many cases, the choice of remedy is far more important than the initial finding of liability. When the case came before Judge Colleen Kollar-Kotelly, damages disappeared from the picture, as did any further talk of breakup. Nor did Judge Kollar-Kotelly attempt to compute the gains that Microsoft derived from illegal practices. Instead, she adopted the simplest and most direct approach, which was to isolate and then enjoin the illegal practices that were possible sources of the problem. Her final decree reflected the solution that the DOJ (which had passed from Democratic to Republican hands after the 2000 presidential election), Microsoft, and many of the states hammered out in extensive negotiations. In an exhaustive opinion, she reviewed the remedial possibilities and then entered a decree that tracked the agreed-upon proposal. Her final judgment might not have pleased the DOJ officials in the Clinton administration, and it certainly did not command the assent of many of the state attorneys general involved. But Judge Kollar-Kotelly had the good sense to follow the roadmap laid down by the substantive determinations of the court of appeals.

Retaliation. Judge Kollar-Kotelly barred Microsoft from retaliating against any OEM that sought to do business with any Microsoft competitor in "developing, distributing, promoting, using, selling, or licensing any software that competes with Microsoft Platform Software or any product or service that distributes or promotes any Non-Microsoft Middleware." The provision covers marketing and shipping goods or services that use middleware from non-Microsoft sources or some alternative operating system. Under the final judgment, all OEM licensees may not only install non-Microsoft icons but may also remove Microsoft icons. Similar options are given for the initial boot sequence. These provisions prevent Microsoft from taking steps to maintain its monopoly over the desktop, like those it had used against Apple and Intel.

The decree contains parallel antiretaliation prohibitions with respect to Internet Service Providers (ISPs) or Independent Hardware Vendors (IHVs) who develop, use, distribute, promote, or support software that competes with Microsoft products. In addition, the decree allows Microsoft to enter into cooperative and promotional arrangements with ISVs and IHVs to test and develop its own products—an exception to a general rule prohibiting Microsoft from tying the sale or licensing of its products to contracting partners who agree to steer clear of non-Microsoft products. Both antiretaliation provisions contain necessary exceptions that allow Microsoft to enforce claims against a contracting partner for ordinary contract breaches (such as nonpayment), so long as that claim is not inconsistent with the final judgment. Parallel rules pertain to intellectual property rights.

Nondiscrimination. A second set of prohibitions imposes a general nondiscrimination obligation on Microsoft in dealing with "covered OEMs," meaning the twenty OEMs with the largest worldwide dollar volume of Windows sales, recalculated annually. The nondiscrimination provision—a common weapon used to counter monopoly power (for example, in utility regulation)—does not track any of the identified violations in *Microsoft III*, but prevents Microsoft from playing favorites with certain cooperative OEMs in an effort to prolong its market dominance.

Nondiscrimination provisions must distinguish between two forms of price discrimination: the "bad" kind that allows for the extraction of monopoly rents, and the "good" kind that allows the supplier to respond to differences in its cost of providing the good or service to its trading partners.[46] Ignore that distinction, and a rule that prevents price discrimination is transmuted into one that mandates unspecified but often hefty cross-subsidies from low-cost to high-cost customers in ways that frustrate the procompetitive goals of the antitrust laws. The 2002 Microsoft consent decree is sensitive to the differences between these two forms of price discrimination. It sensibly allows for price variation between language versions (where the cost per unit could differ with the size of the sales), for reasonable volume discounts (which reflect the lower cost of distribution for large quantities), and for development allowances and similar programs that allow Microsoft to compensate partners who supply it with objectively verifiable market development assistance. Microsoft must offer the same opportunities to all covered OEMs, but with a further proviso that allows it to offer one set of benefits to the ten largest and a second (and lower) rate to the second-tier OEMs. Unfortunately, this provision is not easy to interpret or enforce, and, even with the exceptions, the nondiscrimination rule may block Microsoft from responding to market conditions. (Even the foolish Robinson-Patman Act allows a party to reduce its prices in order to meet competition.)[47] This section will be anticompetitive if read to exclude that option.

Disclosure. The decree requires that "Microsoft shall disclose to ISVs, IHVs, IAPs, ICPs [Internet Content Providers], and OEMs, for the sole purpose of interoperating with the Windows Operating System Product," the APIs and related information that Microsoft uses to interoperate its own middleware with its operating system.[48] It imposes similar obligations and constraints with respect to the protocols that third persons need for interoperating or communicating with Windows. These provisions track Microsoft's common practice of making its APIs available generally because, otherwise, independent software operators could not take advantage of any of the functionality that Windows builds into its operating system.[49] Two points are worth noting. First, the required disclosures are limited *solely* to secure interoperability, and hence do not, and should not, cover protocols that govern server-client communication, or interoperability issues. That restriction has a powerful *pro*competitive bias, for otherwise competitors could incorporate Windows features into their own competing equipment without having to pay license fees. Similarly, Microsoft must license its intellectual property on reasonable and nondiscriminatory terms that "need be no broader than is necessary to ensure" that its licensees can "exercise their options or alternatives expressly provided under this final judgment," but not to use the licensed information for collateral purposes.[50] As with the rest of the 2002 final judgment, this provision does not seek to transform the software industry. It only addresses the most important obstacle to open competition, namely, the inability to hook up on equal terms to Microsoft's operating system.

To see the wisdom of this provision, compare the terms of the Kollar-Kotelly consent decree and those that the European Commission proposed in its March 24, 2004 decision on the same matter. In applying the broad language of article 82 of the European Union,[51] the EC has taken an expansive view of the Microsoft abuse that led it inexorably to impose a more stringent set of remedies. It is easy to unhinge liability from a coherent account of social welfare when the governing provision contains such loose terms as "unfair purchase or selling prices or other unfair trading conditions." The EC decree represents the familiar, if regrettable, situation, where a provision that is intended to promote competition turns out to thwart it. It requires Microsoft to supply "complete and accurate specifications for all the *Protocols* implemented in the *Windows Work Group Server Operating Systems* and that are used by *Windows Work Group Servers*, to deliver file and print services and group and user administrative services including the Windows Domain Controller services, Active Directory services and Group Policy services, to Windows *Work Group Networks*," which it must then make "available to any undertaking having an interest in developing and distributing work group server operating system products," and "on reasonable and non-discriminatory terms, [to] allow [its] use by such undertakings for the purpose of developing and distributing work group server operating system production."[52] This mouthful, in effect, obliges Microsoft to make its data available to other firms not just for purposes of interconnection but for any use at all, including the development of competing work group server operating equipment. In addition, the EC approach permits any licensee to take the information that it so acquires and to license it to the public at large. The only exception to this general rule pertains to trade secrets that would independently entitle them to patent protection.

This is the opposite of sound competition policy. The ability of firms to use Microsoft's trade secrets for any purposes they please allows the information to be published not only in the EU but, necessarily, worldwide. The EC decree thus negates the protective provisions that were carefully worked into the American system. It also creates an implicit cross-subsidy to latecomers to the market, who are allowed to convert Microsoft's property to their own use without any, let alone just, compensation. We are not dealing with a regulation that restricts the way in which the holder of a trade secret can use the information that it has. Rather, we have a rule that allows someone else to use the secret as if it were its own. Under American law, this order would constitute a per se violation of the takings clause, requiring the full compensation for lost value. Finally, the narrow exception carved out in the EC order, pertaining to patentable trade secrets, is wholly inapposite in this context. Of course, trade secret and patent protections are often substitutes for each other, in which case the holder of the property could choose one or the other, but not both. But it has long been established under American law, and the law of everywhere else, that trade secret protection is not limited to material that is patented, but includes all sorts of other materials, including customer lists, for which patent protection would be inappropriate.[53] The contrast between the EC decree and the U.S. disposition could not be more vivid.

Enforcement. The U.S. final judgment contains sensible enforcement provisions. One set of provisions allows the United States to enforce the judgment on its own motion. Another set of provisions creates a joint committee of the states and DOJ to reduce Microsoft's compliance burden. Individual states can sue under the final judgment only after first consulting with both the United States and the joint committee. The final judgment authorizes the creation of an expert and neutral three-person technical committee to oversee Microsoft activities, including powers to interview personnel and examine documents, field complaints, and report to the judge at least every six months. All its work is subject to Microsoft's standard nondisclosure agreement. The final judgment also calls for the appointment of a Microsoft internal compliance officer to educate all Microsoft officers, directors, and employees as to its terms so they can act in accordance with them. The decree expires after five years, but may be extended one time for up to two years "if Microsoft has engaged in a pattern of willful and systematic violations" of its provisions. Microsoft has voluntarily extended the portions applying to protocols for two years.[54]

Challenges to the 2002 Final Judgment

Once the final judgment was entered, several states attacked it for imposing too few obligations on Microsoft. That challenge raises both structural and substantive issues. On the former, the key question is whether the settlement should be controlled by the United States or by any state with a more aggressive antitrust posture.[55] As currently constituted, the antitrust laws allow for both federal and state enforcement in nationwide cases. In most cases that dual jurisdiction will be of little consequence because only one or the other sovereign will see fit to sue. But with dramatic cases like *Microsoft*, state attorneys general will jump eagerly into the fray. If the states prefer relief that is no greater than that sought by the DOJ, their presence does not change the outcome. But just one state's demand for more stringent relief will seek to govern behavior throughout the United States. Its demands will have more profound effects, in the aggregate, outside the state's borders than within it. Given the complexity of the underlying issues, moreover, there is no reason to suppose that the more stringent antitrust relief that one state seeks necessarily works to promote higher levels of market competition. As noted, for example, in connection to tie-ins and disclosure the most aggressive antitrust remedies could easily have anti-competitive consequences. The DOJ could block states from challenging the final judgment in a case to which they are proper parties, but in *Microsoft*, the states had instituted a separate parallel proceeding. Many urged Judge Kollar-Kotelly to impose more stringent obligations on Microsoft. Massachusetts challenged her final judgment in the District of Columbia Court of Appeals, only to lose in a unanimous opinion authored by Judge Douglas Ginsburg.[56]

The substantive objections were raised by protesting states both before Judge Kollar-Kotelly and on the appeal from that decision in *Microsoft IV*. They are also set out in concise and cogent fashion in Herbert Hovenkamp's recent book, *The Antitrust Enterprise*. Hovenkamp opens up his spirited attack by quoting the general objectives of antitrust remedies: to unfetter the market, to terminate the illegal monopoly, to deny the defendant the fruits of its illegal conduct, and to prevent a repetition of the initial wrong. He concludes that none of these goals can be reached under the final judgment.[57] "If so," he writes, "the *Microsoft* case may prove to be one of the great debacles in the history of public antitrust enforcement, snatching defeat from the jaws of victory."[58] That harsh judgment pays insufficient respect to the care and attention both courts gave to their exhaustive review of the case. It systematically downplays the underlying issue of causation, and it wrongly postulates that a perfect competitive solution is attainable in this market.

The basic objective of the 2002 final judgment was to remove any influence that Microsoft's illegal practices might have had on the operation of the PC operating system through the operation of middleware. That objective is perfectly consistent with a single firm's dominant position. As is now well understood, no ideal static competitive solution is possible for network industries where the attractiveness of any software application to both developers and users is heavily dependent on the size of its installed base.[59] Hence, no inference can be drawn about the effectiveness of the 2002 final judgment from the simple observation that Microsoft has retained its dominant position for both servers and the browser, whether conceived as one or two markets. Hovenkamp, therefore, is demanding the impossible by insisting that "the point of assessment down the road is not to ensure that Microsoft has complied with the decree, but that the market is moving toward the competition that the court insisted should be the goal of the antitrust remedy in the first place."[60] That observation repeats the mistake implicit in the wrong characterization of the standard that the purpose of consent decrees generally is to "unfetter" competitive markets. Instead, one should ask whether any anticompetitive practices remain in the market. That is unlikely. The 2002 final judgment addressed all the anticompetitive practices identified in *Microsoft III*. Moreover, Microsoft continues to comply with all the prohibitions imposed in the final judgment pursuant to *Microsoft I*.[61]

More concretely, it is highly unlikely, even under ideal conditions, that any second operating system or browser capable of becoming a general purpose platform will crop up, given the additional cost imposed on software writers who will now have to write for two software platforms instead of one. Hovenkamp notes that, three years after the decree was entered, there has been no market movement to write for "highly competitive alternatives such as Mozilla, Opera, and a revitalized version of Netscape."[62] To be sure, one study suggests a decline of IE market share (on operating systems, not just Windows), from 87 percent in the last quarter of 2002, when the final judgment was entered, to 64 percent in the first quarter of 2005, the last for which data are available. That same study suggests Netscape shares moved from 9 percent to 22 percent during that period.[63] More credible commercial studies show that general populations have remained with IE, whose market share has only recently fallen below 90 percent.[64] But no matter what someone might consider the ideal distribution of market shares, no matter how the data are interpreted, the central point is that right now, none of the offending contractual provisions or business practices remains in play. If 90 percent or even 64 percent is thought too high, it is unlikely that Microsoft's past violations account for the result. Hovenkamp's observation is more consistent with the proposition that any Microsoft competitive edge in its core market is attributable to its own business prowess rather than with some mysterious continued effect of restrictive practices that ended long before these new products reached the market. If anything, the larger market for all computer products cuts in favor of the new entrants, who should be able to achieve some scale economies (on the model of Apple) with a smaller fraction of the underlying market.

Looking backwards, the cumulative evidence on causation does not support an inference that Microsoft's past dominance is largely attributable to its anticompetitive practices. Hovenkamp laments that Microsoft practices, including the use of per-processor licenses banned in the initial decree, resulted in the death of IBM's OS/2. "Microsoft entered into a consent decree that forbade per processor licensing, but by that time the damage was done—OS/2 was virtually dead and never recovered."[65] It is not at all clear, however, that OS/2 was in fact the superior program that would have been adopted without per-processor licenses. IBM was unable to sell many copies of OS/2 on its own machines, when no legal impediments stood in its way. And only a few customers chose to activate the OS/2 program on the Windows PCs that IBM sold—before they dropped the option.[66] Here, as earlier in *United Shoe*, strong customer preferences on price and quality do more than contractual restrictions to keep customer loyalty. And even supposing OS/2 were the superior program, it hardly follows that we would have a pure competitive market today. The need for a single platform could have resulted in the total displacement of Microsoft Windows, so that what would have emerged would have been a market with the same structure, with IBM rather than Microsoft in the dominant position. There are no reasons to believe that this outcome has any better or worse social welfare properties than the present market.

Elsewhere, too, Hovenkamp overrates the effects of restrictive practices. Thus he notes that a dominant firm can help maintain its lofty position "by bundling new elements into the existing system. That is, there is no discrete break between the first and second operating systems, but only a rolling set of upgrades incorporating innovations as they are developed."[67] Further, Hovenkamp suggests that Microsoft "supports" its older systems only for a short period of time, in order to shift its users to the newer versions, and he notes that although many computers and their key components have a useful physical life of ten or twelve years, they receive support for only three or four years.[68] Not so with operating systems, where no such strategy of planned obsolescence is deployed: Microsoft still supports Windows 2000, in 2006.

Again, though, the argument proves unpersuasive even in principle. The firm that decides to limit its support to only three or four years runs serious business risks wholly apart from the antitrust laws. When known by users in advance, the strategy reduces new sales to customers who want the assurance that their products will be supported for a longer period of time. Once the support is withdrawn, moreover, nothing keeps (at least some) users from abandoning Microsoft (or indeed any other supplier) to purchase a rival brand. On the customer side of the market, it is far from clear that anyone wants support for computers, as opposed to refrigerators, for ten or twelve years. The older machines cannot work at the speed of the new ones; they work less well with new applications, and they communicate less well through the Internet with other machines.[69] Perhaps there is some small incentive to shorten (or lengthen) the period of support in an effort to wring some additional monopoly power out of a position. But these strategies are all open to any rival supplier that also enjoys a short-term advantage of working with established customers. One cannot easily fashion an antitrust decree that mandates the type or frequency of upgrades that should be required of Microsoft or anyone else. The 2002 final judgment should be commended for skirting this treacherous terrain.

The same caution applies to Hovenkamp's criticism that the 2002 final judgment contained no provision to prevent Microsoft from commingling Windows and IE Code.[70] Echoing the objectors to the settlement, Hovenkamp urges that some code be ripped out of Windows in order to redress the commingling violation. But Judge Kollar-Kotelly wisely followed the presumption against forcing design changes in the remedial stages of an antitrust decree. The point was especially potent because code removal was not needed to remedy this particular violation: "The evidence presented to the Court indicates that the ability to remove end-user access to any commingled functionality would sufficiently address the anticompetitive aspect of the conduct and would prove far less disruptive to consumers and industry participants."[71]

A complementary remedy to the forced removal of code from the basic program would, in Hovenkamp's words, require "Microsoft to auction off nonexclusive licenses of its Windows source code to four or five purchasers, each of which could then develop its own version of Windows, creating a competitive network environment."[72] That proposal received short shrift from Judge Kollar-Kotelly, and for good reason. Contrary to the logic of network industries, it assumes that a competitive solution with many firms is, in fact, more efficient than a single system. The judge stressed that software developers have a real interest in avoiding fragmentation of software platforms, which would require them to write multiple versions of the same program. In particular, she rejected a proposal from the states that would have required Microsoft to remove code from its operating system, to wit:

> Microsoft shall not, in any Windows Operating System Product . . . it distributes . . . bind any Microsoft Middleware Product to the Windows Operating System unless Microsoft also has available to license, upon the request of any Covered OEM licensee or Third-Party Licensee, and supports both directly and indirectly, an otherwise identical but "unbound" Windows Operating System Product.

In Judge Kollar-Kotelly's view, the evidence suggested that this proposal "would hinder, or even destroy Microsoft's ability to provide a consistent API set."[73] The court of appeals gave a full-throated endorsement to her position. "Far from abusing its discretion," the court wrote, "the district court, by remedying the anticompetitive effect of commingling, went to the heart of the problem Microsoft had created, and it did so without intruding itself into the design and engineering of the Windows operating system. We say, Well done!"[74]

The sorry history of ambitious consent decrees cuts against Hovenkamp's insistence on more draconian remedies. The structural remedy adopted in *United Shoe* is most on point because that decree was entered after (predictably) the more limited remedies on specific contractual provisions did little to change overall market structure. But far from proving that anticompetitive forces were still at work, *United Shoe* only showed that the natural efficiencies from dealing with a single supplier remain critical even after all exclusive-dealing provisions and their implicit surrogates (long-leases, service contracts) are excised. No one would want to use these decisions as role models for the future. Similarly, the *Bell System* breakup, both in terms of Judge Greene's decree and the unfortunate experience of the 1996 Telecommunications Act, failed so expensively precisely because the required sale of unbundled network elements at state-determined prices created the treacherous shoals of implicit cross-subsidies that Judge Kollar-Kotelly's 2002 final judgment carefully avoided.

Solutions that involve the use of nonlegal means fare no better. Hovenkamp mentions the sale of excess government aluminum capacity to Kaiser or Reynolds, but not Alcoa—the previous dominant player—in order to create more competition. But what may work in nonnetwork industries lacks an analog in a network context. Hovenkamp thinks that the *Alcoa* case provides an argument for government use of open-source software to offset the monopoly dominance of Microsoft.[75] That, though, looks more like a decision to buy from Kaiser or Reynolds after the initial sale, even if their prices are higher than Alcoa's. The proposal is not tied to any underlying violation of the antitrust laws. Moreover, it advances the social interest only if the current market structure is the result of anti-competitive behaviors, not of the network externalities that drive most users to single operating systems. In addition, we can identify inefficiencies of the sort that might not be found in the sale of excess government assets to Kaiser and Reynolds, to the exclusion of Alcoa. In particular, government agencies would have to bear in at least some cases higher costs, while reducing the size of an installed base that might spur greater innovation for software developers that write for Windows. Open-source software has real advantages over proprietary systems in some instances, which it should be allowed to exploit. But if it has offsetting disadvantages, only market institutions can sort out the relative magnitude of the pluses and minuses.

The final judgment is due to expire of its own terms in November 2007, except insofar as Microsoft has extended it for two years to cover those aspects touching on server operations. What next? Consistent with his negative evaluation of the decree, Herbert Hovenkamp concludes that, as a matter of public policy,

> the legal wheels turn far too slowly. By the time each round of *Microsoft* litigation had produced a 'cure,' the victim was already dead. This makes it vitally important that settlements such as the one in *Microsoft* contain a clause that permits a court to retain jurisdiction and assess the future.[76]

That recommendation, however, seems incorrect on both legal and policy grounds.

The wheels of litigation do grind slowly, and continuous judicial supervision under a consent decree reduces the time needed for legal enforcement of any particular provision. Speed, however, should count on both sides of the ledger. Even the short time that is needed to respond to demands from a district court judge or a technical committee—even where there is no antitrust violation at all—matters. In an industry with very short product cycles, any diversion of resources to the oversight process could slow down innovation by critical days, weeks, or months. The built-in drag will happen with the ablest of judges and the most diligent of technical committees. It will be compounded by imperfections in either process. While the advantage to competitors is manifest, the gains to competition are far less clear.

Hovenkamp seems willing to bear these costs because he misapprehends the role of judicial oversight. His initial mistake in thinking that the perfect decree in the *Microsoft* litigation will produce a competitive market leaves him uneasy about Microsoft's ability to maintain its dominant position, notwithstanding its compliance with the substantive provisions of the decree. And his dismissal of all the genuine causal difficulties—the victim is "dead"— lead him to overstate the market significance of the anticompetitive practices relative to lawful ones. In consequence, he overstates the social return that derives from the punctual enforcement of the present decree.

Nor, it appears, has he accurately predicted Microsoft's response to the entire episode. Its original strategy during the 1990s was to fight every application of the antitrust laws to its operations even though the basic case against it rested on traditional principles. The effect of that strategy was to exaggerate the importance of the various contractual provisions that Microsoft worked so hard to protect, and to make it appear that market efficiencies had little to do with its continued marketplace success. The company's newer response yields on the liability issue but works hard to shape the appropriate remedy. That attitude need not be expressed only in litigation. It could also take place as stated firm policy in the sensible effort to forestall further litigation.

And with a change in the legal guard at Microsoft, just that conciliatory and sensible policy has been introduced. On July 19, 2006, Brad Smith, Microsoft's general counsel, outlined Microsoft's new business posture in a speech before the National Press Club in Washington, D.C., dealing with the impendent launch of the next generation Vista Operating System.[77] Nobody could say these remarks represent the attitude of a company that is determined to live in a fortified bunker. Rather, its stated overall objective is that Microsoft is committed to designing Windows to make it easy to install non-Microsoft applications and to configure Windows-based PCs to use non-Microsoft programs instead of, or in addition to, Windows features.[78] Smith articulated a variety of rules that are intended to promote access and transparency so that even competitors can build on the Microsoft platform. In effect, the rules in question recognize the force of the criticism against Microsoft's exclusivity policy and seek to respond appropriately. The result should, moreover, be good all the way round, for the greater access to the platform should also expand the effective market for the Vista Operating System.

It would be a general overstatement to think that the articulation of these principles counts as the creation of a legally enforceable contract that binds Microsoft to the rest of the world. But the point hardly matters, because of the massive political and antitrust risk that would follow from any deviation from these without some strong business justification. There is little doubt that these principles are in part intended to deal with the expected life of the consent decree, which reaches its five-year break renewal point in November 2007. The stronger the voluntary compliance, the weaker the need for any oversight.

Even without the articulation of these principles, the language of the 2002 final judgment is not easily amenable to its casual extension, as shown below.

Termination

Unlike most open-ended consent decrees, the *Microsoft* decree addresses the subject of termination specifically as follows:

> A. Unless this Court grants an extension, this Final Judgment will expire on the fifth anniversary of the date it is entered by the Court [November 12, 2007].

B. In any enforcement proceeding in which the Court has found that Microsoft has engaged in a pattern of willful and systematic violations, the Plaintiff may apply to the Court for a one-time extension of this Final Judgment of up to two years, together with such other relief as the Court may deem appropriate.[79]

This provision does not impose a perpetual decree of the *Swift & Co.* variety. The rigidities of that approach have led to a commendable shortening of the enforcement window. The district court need not make a finding that all the terms of the 2002 final judgment should be left in place unless Microsoft can show that it is subject to some grievous wrong, aggravated by the change of circumstances. Nor does the decree give the DOJ or the states a leg up in seeking an extension of the final judgment. The initial phrase ("unless this court grants an extension") does not place any special burden of proof on Microsoft. Quite the opposite: Even when taken alone, the natural sense of the clause is that the ordinary rules of motion practice should govern. The plaintiffs must make out some case for an extension. This natural reading gains added power in light of the specific language allowing a one-time extension in the event of "a pattern of willful and systematic violations" of the final judgment. It would be most odd to allow any longer extension under clause (A) in cases where there has been no pattern of willful and systematic violations. And while clause (B) allows for the addition of "such other relief as the Court may deem appropriate," *no* such power is granted under clause (A). Nor, on a sensible reading, does the additional relief encompass a freewheeling revision of the final judgment in order to vindicate Hovenkamp's ideal of perfect competition. It only contemplates additional sanctions if Microsoft acts in violation of the substantive obligations that have already been established under other provisions of the final judgment.

In this legal framework, the case for a renewal of the final judgment is weak in light of the post-2002 events. Ultimately, of course, the question of extension involves some use of judicial discretion. But it seems clear that clause (B) is quite out of the picture, for whatever violations of this final judgment that have taken place have resulted from Microsoft's lack of perfect management control and have been corrected quickly upon detection by senior management.[80] So the only issue left is a generalized extension under clause (A). In looking at this question, it is worth noting that the final judgment in *Microsoft I* expired in early 2002, but its central prohibitions have been observed without incident in the past four years. Even without that final judgment in place, the legal principles on exclusive dealing that related to such matters as per-processor licenses are too well-established to admit any doubt. Microsoft has complied with the first decree, without making any effort to challenge the substantive judgments of *Microsoft I*. A fresh lawsuit could be quickly decided in accordance with its principles even though that final judgment is expired. Tellingly, none has been needed.

The same logic applies here. All the substantive principles remain in place. A violation of the applicable rules will necessarily involve public acts, and not the concealed offenses found in price-fixing cases. It should be a straightforward matter to see whether the applications of non-Microsoft vendors work as well as Microsoft's. Enforcement of the relevant principles should not be in doubt even after the shackles of the 2002 final judgment are removed.

Nor, as the Smith speech makes evident, does Microsoft have any business incentive to violate the terms of the final judgment. As noted earlier, the anticompetitive provisions that were enjoined in *Microsoft I* and *III* had, as best one can tell, relatively small effects on the configuration of the market for both operating systems and browsers. There is no reason why that should change in the future as the market continues to evolve away from the industry conditions that gave rise to this dispute in the first place. It would be foolish for Microsoft to invite public rebuke and government action by taking notorious steps that have already been held anticompetitive in multiple cases. Finally, the market has shifted. In the past four years, open-source software, now backed by a powerful IBM-led consortium, has established itself as a permanent player in the operating system market, especially with respect to complex processes. Indeed, one of the advantages is that "the complete Linux operating system is freely downloadable over the Internet."[81] Apple, led in part by its iPOD, has been able to expand its market share. With its pending switch to Intel-compatible processors and other industry-standard hardware, the gap between Apple and PC prices will continue to shrink. In consequence, the cost of shifting to non-Microsoft operating systems is reduced. As various applications and files are ever easier to convert from one system to another, shifting costs are further reduced. As storage capacity continues to expand, an ever-greater fraction of the population routinely carries more than one program for any use.[82] New forces, such as Google, loom large in the search market, and Google has (through g-mail and its own instant message service) moved into adjacent areas. New entry from unanticipated sources offers the most powerful form of market discipline.

5

Lessons Learned

The common law has always been concerned with the issues of monopoly. Yet, for the most part, it was content with relatively modest interventions in the marketplace. The standard common-law rule held that courts would in general not enforce contracts that were made in restraint of trade—which did nothing to punish the various cartelization and market-division devices that self-interested firms could generate for themselves. It did impose duties of service on common carriers, which required them to take all comers on reasonable and nondiscriminatory terms. Yet, in both these contexts, it tended to address obvious violations without seeking to mount the massive forms of antitrust litigation and ratemaking hearings that are so characteristic of the modern law.

These new developments received their impetus with the rise of industrialization in the post–Civil War period, when major improvements in technology and the massive aggregations of capital tested the traditional view. The usual populist view at the time was that these vast forces tended to stifle competition, for which regulation was the answer. In many instances, however, the situation tended to be the opposite. The new forms of business allowed for the introduction of superior technologies, communications, and transportation that displaced the static monopolies that had held onto their local power for too long.[1] In many modern circles it is, to say the least, unfashionable to express doubtful views about the role of antitrust law, but it is to me an open question whether the entire enterprise has been worth the candle, given the errors of both under- and overenforcement. There is no need, however, to take an all-or-nothing position on this issue in light of the many intermediate positions available. One obvious approach is to heed caution when the attention shifts from liability to damages. It is just on this point that the history of final judgments in antitrust cases, whether by settlement or litigation, kicks in. The broad sweep of antitrust history shows that under any sensible standard of social welfare, excessive ambition generally proves counterproductive. It is relatively easy to implement sound legal regimes that block the continued operation of a cartel. It is much more difficult to construct equally effective regimes to master the murky world of unilateral practices. For public officials and private parties in the antitrust arena, that history holds several more specific lessons.

Let Private Firms Engage in the Unilateral Surrender of Unilateral Restrictions. One point stands out more than any other: The moment some specialized contract provision that speaks about ties or exclusivity is challenged, the best advice to the firm is to abandon it forthwith. In practice, a firm's success in adopting programs that are intended to bind its customers usually arises from the fact that its goods and services work more cheaply and reliably when supplied in combination rather than isolation. To keep the disputed contractual restrictions in place is to invite the suspicion that where there is smoke there is always fire—whereupon virtually all ill-fated consequences to competitors may come to be attributed to form restrictions rather than the underlying product advantage. Remove the provision, and the potentially explosive form of liability is removed, usually with little or no loss in market share or profitability. Whether you are United Shoe with tough lease provisions or Microsoft with specific rules on default browsers or icon placement, surrender and do so quickly.

Let the Regulatory Punishment Fit the Offense. Blunt legal instruments often injure innocent bystanders. We need to avoid that damage by making sure that the punishment fits the crime. It is always a mistake to posit that those guilty of one offense have really committed many others so that prompt intervention is needed to prevent a repetition. That conviction led to breakups in the aluminum and shoe industries, among others, without any beneficial results. Sometimes firms come by their dominant positions because they have done things right, even if they are not quite clear just how that happened. (Business executives are better at responding to immediate incentives in ways that make sense than they are at articulating the reasons for what they do.) Courts should not punish folks for what they have not done, on a mere suspicion of multiple transgressions fueled by the occasional injudicious remark. Government lawyers should not—in the fashion of the Wilson administration—force defendants to cave with respect to wrongs they have not committed in order to survive punishment for the wrongs they have committed. The goal is not to maximize punishment but to maximize social welfare.

Use One System of Regulation, Not Two. While there is only one way *not* to regulate, there are many ways in which to regulate, and these often work at cross-purposes. The wisdom is to keep the lines of regulation as simple and clean as possible, so that one problem has only one regulator. That lesson became abundantly clear when no one could figure out the respective domains of the FCC and the antitrust laws in dealing with the breakup of the Bell System. Once a direct form of regulation deals with the monopoly issue, antitrust law is, at best, redundant. If the government agency can fix rates, the danger of monopoly has in most cases been effectively countered. Even if it has not, the addition of a second, erratic form of governance will scramble the lines of communication. And, as noted, the court's limited jurisdiction poses a constant risk that a consent decree will govern one firm but not its direct competitor, thereby skewing the competitive field without benefiting consumers. Why create opportunities for legal arbitrage? Do it once, and do it right.

Recognize That New Entry Beats Comprehensive Regulation. The pace of litigation is always slower than the pace of technical and business innovation. While much ink has been spilled on the "right" modification standard of long-term consent decrees, judicial modification of consent decrees is slow and awkward no matter what the legal standard. In case after case, competitive juices produced new technologies that undercut established businesses by going around their traditional mode of operation. High prices create an umbrella over new entrants that only hastens their arrival on the scene. The great risk of regulation is that it will so hamstring the incumbent that the new entrant will have an unfair advantage, solely because it does not have to labor under restrictions that have outlived their usefulness long before some court decides whether or not to modify or terminate the decree. This market dynamic suggests that the large risk lies in regulating too tightly, not too loosely. And, fortunately, there are signs that courts and prosecutors are getting the message that tough consent decrees often do more for inefficient competitors than for diligent consumers. Consent decrees now often contain five-year maximums, as do some final judgments (recall *Microsoft*), and the Antitrust Division has streamlined its review process for considering modification or termination requests.[2] These are good ways to avoid sclerosis.

Less Is More. Remedies can be too severe, too lax, or just right. Some error will always creep in. Which way will it cut? In the antitrust context, overenforcement is much more dangerous than underenforcement. There is the initial risk that the new set of restrictions will operate in an anticompetitive fashion against the incumbent. And it is always more expensive to do more than it is to do less. In terms of social utility, less enforcement results in more social improvement. Keep it simple, and you are more likely to do it right.

Appendix

History of Antitrust Consent Decrees

Defendant	Date	Notes
Otis Elevator	1906	First antitrust consent decree.
Alcoa	1912, 1945, 2000	*1912*: Required to divest interest in Canadian subsidiary and terminate contract with two chemical firms; *1945*: Prohibited participation in mergers/collusive agreements and discrimination against fabricator competitor, selling ingot; *2000*: Required divestiture of an aluminum manufacturing facility.
Swift	1920	Prohibited packers to handle/own interest in specified food categories; restricted participation in retail meat markets; required to divest interest in retail meat markets, stockyards, public cold storages, market newspaper/journals, terminal railroads.
Eastman Kodak Co.	1921, 1954	*1921*: Enjoined Kodak from prohibiting dealers from freely selling competitors' goods; *1954*: Enjoined Kodak from tying the sale of color film to processing of color film; contained conditional divestiture of 50 percent of color film facilities after seven years if Kodak did not prove enough competition in industry.
Chrysler, Ford Motor Company	1938	Prohibited from affiliating with any consumer financing company.

(continued on next page)

(continued from previous page)

Defendant	Date	Notes
Paramount Pictures et al.	1940, 1949	*1940*: Multiple provisions that govern picture licensing, block booking, and blind selling provisions; provisions prevented run and clearance designations; curbed extensions of affiliated circuits; *1949*: Ordered five major movie distributors to divest movie theatre holdings, but did not order them to break up.
ASCAP, BMI	1941, 1950, 1966	Modifications in 1960, 1994, and 2000. See table 1, in chapter 1.
AT&T	1956, 1982	*1956*: Ordered AT&T to divest non-tele-activities, barring those related to national defense; Divided *1982*: Broke AT&T up into Baby Bells.
United Shoe Machinery	1953	Prohibited United Shoe from designing lease/sale terms to make it more advantageous to lease versus buy.
Empro Corporation	1954	Agreed to give consent to any entity that sought to import toiletries manufactured under Empro's trademarks or trade names of foreign affiliates.
IBM	1956	Multiple provisions included: requirement for IBM to offer computers for sale, not just for lease; to license patents; to establish separate subsidiary for service bureau business; to terminate exclusive dealings with raw materials of tabulating cards. Also contained conditional divestiture provision.
Torrington	1957	Prohibited from obtaining assets of machine needle production companies; prohibited from restricting competition in machine needle market through exclusive agreements.

(continued on next page)

Defendant	Date	Notes
Safeway	1957	Limited the ability to reduce prices if such a price reduction would have a severe impact on competition.
United Fruit	1958	Enjoined from entering into exclusive dealing arrangements, from acquiring or entering into business with competitors that involved importing bananas into United States, among other predatory and monopolistic practices.
Northern Pacific Co. & Northwestern Improvement Co.	1959	Prohibited from compelling lessees to ship freight by Northern Pacific Railway or other specified railway company.
General Motors	1965	Enjoined from entering into exclusive supply contractors with other bus manufacturing or operating companies; required to sell buses and bus engines/transmissions to any operator or manufacturer; certain provisions governing reasonable royalty licensing.
Bank of Virginia	1966	Prohibited from exclusive provisions in its contracts that restrict members from dealing with other credit service plans.
Blue Chip Trading Stamps	1967	Reorganized the ownership of Blue Chip; Prohibited Blue Chip companies from refusing service to retailers for a variety of reasons that restrained trade and monopolized the trading stamp business.
Northern Natural Gas Co.	1970	Prohibited from entering contracts that gave Northern Natural Gas the option to supply volumes of natural gas that exceeded the maximum volumes initially stated in the contracts.

(continued on next page)

(continued from previous page)

Defendant	Date	Notes
Bunge Corporation	1970	Prohibited from conditioning use of grain elevators on the agreement of customers to Bunge's choice of personnel; prohibited from restricting elevator use to those using particular stevedores.
Hercules Inc.	1981	Prevented from colluding with nondomestic "rivals" of industrial nitrocellulose.
Electronic Payment Systems	1994	Multiple provisions that prohibited EPS from restricting ability of depository institution to obtain branded ATM network access; prevented EPS from compelling banks to buy data processing services as precondition of being on MAC ATM network.
Microsoft	1994	Prohibited restrictive licensing agreements: enjoined from per-processor licenses, requiring lump-sum payments, tying other Microsoft products to licensing certain operating systems, requiring purchasing a minimum number of operating systems, requiring software application developers to sign restrictive nondisclosure agreements, and requiring license agreements in excess of one year at a time.
Waste Management of Georgia Inc., Waste Management of Savannah, Waste Management of Louisiana, and Waste Management Inc.	1996	Governs Waste Management's contract that hurt small trash haulers; contains provisions that restrict contract length, renewal scheme, and "right to compete" clauses.
Browning-Ferris Industries of Iowa Inc., Browning-Ferris Industries of Tennessee Inc., and Browning-Ferris Industries Inc.	1996	Governs Browning-Ferris's contract scheme that restricts small trash haulers from market participation; contains provisions that restrict contract length, renewal scheme, and "right to compete" clauses.

(continued on next page)

Defendant	Date	Notes
Intel	1999	Prohibits Intel from regulatory action against customers over IP disputes (as in cases of Compaq, Digital, and Intergraph).
AOL/Time Warner	2000	Requires AOL/Time Warner to provide rival ISPs with access to its cable systems.

Notes

Introduction

1. American Bar Association Antitrust Section, *Antitrust Law Developments*, 3d ed. (Chicago: American Bar Association, 1992), 569–70; American Bar Association Section of Antitrust Law, *Antitrust Law Developments*, 2d ed. (Chicago: American Bar Association, 1984), 361.

2. See, for example, Barry C. Lynn, "Breaking The Chain: The Antitrust Case Against Wal-Mart," *Harper's Magazine* (July 2006).

3. See, for example, *LePage's Inc. v. 3M (Minnesota Mining and Manufacturing Co.)*, 324 F3d 141, 151–52 (3d Cir 2003) (en banc), cert denied, 542 U.S. 952 (2004) (allowing bundling claim when no constituent products sold at below cost); *Weyerhaeuser Co. v. Ross-Simmons Hardwood Co.*, 411 F.3d 1030 (9th Cir. 2005), cert granted, 126 S. Ct. 2965 (2006) (allowing predation claims against a potential seller who was alleged to pay too much for supplies to block out competitor from market).

Chapter 1: Theoretical Foundations

1. *United States v. Atlantic Refining Co.*, 360 U.S. 19, 22–23 (1960).

2. The central provision is 16 U.S.C. 15(e), entitled, "Public Interest Determination":

> (1) Before entering any consent judgment proposed by the United States under this section, the court shall determine that the entry of such judgment is in the public interest. For the purpose of such determination, the court shall consider—

> (A) the competitive impact of such judgment, including termination of alleged violations, provisions for enforcement and modification, duration of relief sought, anticipated effects of alternative remedies actually considered, whether its terms are ambiguous, and any other competitive considerations bearing upon the adequacy of such judgment that the court deems necessary to a determination of whether the consent judgment is in the public interest; and

(B) the impact of entry of such judgment upon competition in the relevant market or markets, upon the public generally and individuals alleging specific injury from the violations set forth in the complaint including consideration of the public benefit, if any, to be derived from a determination of the issues at trial.

More recently, the Act has been modified in ways that appear to increase the level of scrutiny that district courts should apply, but it is unclear by how much when the government's determination is contested by an outside party. See, e.g. *United States of America v. SBC Communications, Inc. & BellSouth Corp.*, Civil Action No. 00-2073 (PLF), http://www.usdoj.gov/atr/cases/f206000/206009.htm (October 13, 2004).

3. *United States v. Swift & Co.*, 286 U.S. 106, 114 (1932) (Cardozo, J.).

4. 286 U.S. 106, 119 (1932).

5. *Rufo v. Imates of the Suffolk County Jail*, 502 U.S. 367, 379–82 (1992).

6. See, for example, Bernard T. Shen, "Comment, From Jail Cell to Cellular Communication: Should the *Rufo* Standard Be Applied to Antitrust and Commercial Consent Decrees?" *Northwestern University Law Review* 90 (Summer 1996): 1781.

7. See, for example, *Bellevue Manor Associates v. United States*, 165 F.3d 1249, 1255 (2d. Cir. 1999), and cases cited, ibid., 1255, note 5. For an earlier adoption of the more flexible standard in antitrust cases, see *United States v. Eastman Kodak*, 63 F.3d 95 (2d. Cir. 1995).

8. See, for example, Michael McConnell, "Why Hold Elections? Using Consent Decrees to Insulate Policies from Political Change," *University of Chicago Legal Forum* (1987): 295–325; Ross Sandler and David Schoenbrod, *Democracy by Decree* (New Haven, Yale University Press, 2003).

9. See, for example, Philip E. Areeda and Herbert Hovenkamp, *Antitrust Law*, 2d ed. (New York: Aspen Law and Business, 2000): 261–64, for a brief discussion of the issue which favored the flexible standard.

10. This describes a general tendency, not an inevitability; defendants may occasionally accept punishment for antitrust violations they did not commit. For a striking illustration see the *Swift* case, discussed on pages 22–29.

11. *Ford Motor Co. v. United States*, 405 U.S. 562, 577 (1972).

12. *United States v. United Shoe Mach. Corp.*, 391 U.S. 244, 250 (1968); *United States v. Grinnell Corp.*, 384 U.S. 563, 577 (1966).

13. For the literature on this subject, see, for example, Randall R. Bovbjerg, Frank A. Sloan, and James F. Blumstein, "Valuing Life and Limb in Tort: Scheduling 'Pain and Suffering,'" *Northwestern University Law Review* 83 (Summer 1989): 908, 923–24; David Friedman, "What Is 'Fair Compensation' For Death or Injury?" *International Review of Law and Economics* 2, no. 1 (June 1982): 81–93; Samuel Rea, "Lump-Sum Versus Periodic Damage Awards," *Journal of Legal Studies* 10, no. 1 (January 1981): 131–54.

14. For a general discussion, see E. Allen Farnsworth, *Contracts*, 2d ed. (New York: Aspen Law and Business, 1990), chapter 12. The classic article (in two parts) on the distinctions is Lon L. Fuller and William R. Perdue Jr., "The Reliance Interest in Contract Damages: 1," *Yale Law Journal* 46, no. 1 (November 1936): 52–96, and Lon L. Fuller and William R. Perdue Jr., "The Reliance Interest in Contract Damages: 2," *Yale Law Journal* 46, no. 3 (January 1937): 373–420.

15. See Farnsworth, *Contracts*, 849, 864 for the various equitable rules.

16. Ibid., 860–61.

17. Ibid., 855–56.

18. In the leading case of *Lumley v. Wagner*, the famous opera singer Johanna Wagner was enjoined from singing at the Royal Italian Opera, Covent Garden, when she was under contract with Lumley to sing exclusively at Her Majesty's Theatre London. 1 DeG. M. & G. 604, 42 Eng. Rep. 687 (Ch. 1852). See also the companion case of *Lumley v. Gye*, 118 Eng. Rep. 749 (KB 1853).

19. See, for example, *Hansen v. Independent School District No. 1*, 98 P.2d 959 (1939) (allowing night games on the school's athletic fields, but only on condition that the defendant controlled lighting, terminated the games at a reasonable hour, and limited neighborhood parking).

20. Richard A. Epstein, "Private Property and the Public Domain: The Case of Anti-Trust Law," in *Ethics, Economics and the Law, Nomos XXIV*, ed. J. Pennock and J. Chapman (New York: New York University Press, 1982), 48.

21. The two sections read:

> Sec. 1. Every contract, combination in the form of trust or otherwise, or conspiracy, in restraint of trade or commerce among the several States, or with foreign nations, is hereby declared to be illegal. Every person who shall make any such contract or engage in any such combination or conspiracy, shall be deemed guilty of a misdemeanor, and, on conviction thereof, shall be punished by fine not exceeding five thousand dollars, or by imprisonment not exceeding one year, or by both said punishments, in the discretion of the court.

> Sec. 2. Every person who shall monopolize, or attempt to monopolize, or combine or conspire with any other person, or persons, to monopolize any part of the trade or commerce among the several States, or with foreign nations, shall be deemed guilty of a misdemeanor, and, on conviction thereof, shall be punished by fine not exceeding five thousand dollars, or by imprisonment not exceeding one year, or by both said punishments, in the discretion of the court.

22. For an example of the former see *Blomkest Fertilizer Inc. v. Potash Corporation of Saskatchewan*, 203 F.3d 1028 (8th Cir. 2000). For a justly negative assessment of the weak opinion, see Herbert Hovenkamp, *The Antitrust Enterprise: Principle and*

Execution (Cambridge, Mass.: Harvard University Press, 2006), 134–35. I am sad to report that I was losing counsel for the plaintiff in my one litigation foray. For an example of the latter, see *Twombly v. Bell Atlantic*, 313 F. Supp. 2d 174 (S.D.N.Y. 2003) (dismissing case on a judgment on the pleadings), rev'd 425 F.3d 99 (2d Cir. 2005), cert granted, 126 S. Ct. 2965. For my critique of this case, with an aside in Blomkest, see Richard A. Epstein, *Motions to Dismiss Antitrust Cases: Separating Fact from Fantasy*, AEI-Brookings Joint Center for Regulatory Studies, March 2006, http://www.aei-brookings.org/admin/authorpdfs/page.php?id= 1262&PHPSES-SID=9b61ad4aeddfd8960ab71446f4432234 (accessed November 6, 2006).

23. See *Mitchel v. Reynolds*, 1 P. Wms. 181, 24 Eng. Rep. 347 (House of Lords, Eng., 1711). The problem is still more acute because one cheaper, albeit less effective, way to attack cartels is for courts simply to refuse to enforce any contracts in restraint of trade, even if they do not allow suits at the instance of the state or private purchasers.

24. I develop this theme in Richard A. Epstein, "Monopoly Dominance or Level Playing Field? The New Antitrust Paradox," *University of Chicago Law Review* 72 (Winter 2005): 49–72.

25. Philip Areeda and Donald F. Turner, "Predatory Pricing and Related Practices Under Section 2 of the Sherman Act," *Harvard Law Review* 88 (February 1975): 697–733, critiqued in Frank H. Easterbrook, "Predatory Strategies and Counterstrategies," *University of Chicago Law Review* 48 (Spring 1981): 263–337.

26. For discussion, see *Matsushita Electric Industrial Co. Ltd. v. Zenith Radio Corp*, 475 US 574, 588 (1986).

27. For the English origins of this rule see *Allnut v. Inglis*, 104 Eng. Rep. 206 (K.B. 1810); for an account of this development, see Richard A. Epstein, *Principles for a Free Society: Reconciling Individual Liberty with the Common Good* (New York: Perseus Books, 1998), 279–318.

28. For my discussion of this point, see Epstein, "Monopoly Dominance or Level Playing Field?" p. 49.

Chapter 2: Case Studies

1. Robert Crandall and Clifford Winston, "Does Antitrust Policy Improve Consumer Welfare? Assessing the Evidence," *Journal of Economic Perspectives* 17, no. 4 (Fall 2003): 3–26.

2. *Standard Oil Company of New Jersey v. United States*, 221 U.S. 1 (1911).

3. John S. McGee, "Predatory Price Cutting: The Standard Oil (N.J.) Case," *Journal of Law and Economics* 1 (October 1958): 137–69.

4. 148 F.2d 416 (2d Cir. 1945).

5. 334 U.S. 131 (1948).

6. Ibid., 143–44.

7. Ibid., 171.

8. For a contemporaneous discussion see "Comment, The Packer Consent Decree," *Yale Law Journal* 42, no. 1 (November 1932): 81–94. For a later analysis of the meatpackers' joint practices and the long-term effects of the decree on their core businesses, see Richard J. Arnould, "Changing Patterns of Concentration in American Meat Packing, 1880–1963," *Business History Review* 45, no. 1 (Spring 1971): 18-34, which notes that the long-term decline of the meatpackers' power was only partially attributable to the decree. The article does not discuss restrictions on entry into collateral markets.

9. *United States v. Swift and Co.*, 286 U.S. 106, 110 (1932).

10. *Swift*, 286 U.S., 110.

11. Ibid., 111 (italics added).

12. "Comment, The Packer Consent Decree," 81, 84–85.

13. See Peter C. Carstenson, "How to Assess the Impact of Antitrust on the American Economy: Examining History or Theorizing," *Iowa Law Review* 74 (July 1989): 1175–1217, 1208.

14. *Swift*, 286 U.S., 106.

15. Ibid., 111. See also *Swift & Co. v. United States*, 276 U.S. 311, 320 (1928).

16. *Swift*, 276 U.S. 311 (1928); *United States v. California Cooperative Canneries*, 279 U.S. 553 (1929).

17. "Comment, The Packer Consent Decree," 81, 92–93.

18. *Swift*, 286 U.S., 113.

19. *Swift*, 286 U.S., 116–17.

20. The changes were very substantial: "In 1920 there were in the United States approximately 15,000 regular chain grocery stores, and of that number approximately 1,200 had meat departments, while by 1929 this number had grown to 60,000 stores of which about 15,800 contained fresh meat departments"; "Comment, The Packer Consent Decree," 81, 88.

21. *Swift*, 286 U.S., 118.

22. Ibid., 119.

23. Ibid., 120–21.

24. Ibid., 121.

25. Ibid., 122.

26. Ibid., 122.

27. Ibid., 123.

28. See Janet L. Avery, "The Struggle over Performing Rights to Music: *BMI and ASCAP v. Cable Television*," *Hastings Communications and Entertainment Law Journal* 14, no. 1 (Fall 1991): 47–84. Michael A. Einhorn, "Intellectual Property and Antitrust: Music Performing Rights in Broadcasting," *Columbia Journal of Law and the Arts* 24, no. 1 (Summer 2001): 349–68; Randal C. Picker, "Unbundling Scope-of-Permission Goods: When Should We Invest in Reducing Entry Barriers?" *University of Chicago Law Review* 72, no. 1 (Winter 2005): 189, 192–96; Noel Hillman, "Intractable Consent: A Legislative Solution to the Problem of Aging Consent Decrees in *United*

States v. ASCAP and *United States v. BMI*," *Fordham Intellectual Property, Media and Entertainment Law Journal* 8 (Spring 1998): 733–71.

29. See, for example, *Broadcast Music Inc. v. Columbia Broadcasting System Inc.* 441 U.S. 1, 5 (1979); American Society of Composers, Authors, and Publishers (ASCAP), "About ASCAP," http://www.ascap.com/about (accessed November 7, 2005); BMI, "About BMI," http://www.bmi.com/about/ (accessed November 7, 2005).

30. *Broadcast Music Inc. v. Columbia Broadcasting System Inc.*, 441 U.S. 1 (1979).

31. For a clear account of the different sort of licenses, relied on here, see Einhorn, "Intellectual Property and Antitrust," and *Broadcast Music*, 441 U.S., 8–12.

32. See American Society of Composers, Authors, and Publishers (ASCAP), "Frequently Asked Questions about General Licensing," http://www.ascap.com/licensing/generalfaq.html (accessed November 6, 2005), noting that ASCAP "has over a hundred different licenses and rate schedules"; BMI, "Licensing," http://www.bmi.com/licensing/ (accessed December 21, 2005).

33. Einhorn, "Intellectual Property and Antitrust," 350.

34. Picker, "Unbundling Scope-of-Permission Goods," 189, 192.

35. Einhorn, "Intellectual Property and Antitrust," notes that different members of writing teams could belong to different organizations. In principle, this should allow for some overlap between the two lists.

36. *United States v. ASCAP*, 1950–1951 Trade Cases, para. 62,595 (SDNY 1950); *United States v. BMI*, 1966-1 Trade Cas. (CCH) para. 71, 941 (S.D.N.Y. 1966).

37. Einhorn, "Intellectual Property and Antitrust," 1, 8.

38. Ibid.

39. Ibid., 18.

40. Hillman, "Intractable Consent," 733, 742.

41. Einhorn, "Intellectual Property and Antitrust," 1, 14 (discussing the different weighting formulas).

42. *Buffalo Broadcasting Co. v. American Soc'y of Composers, Authors & Publishers*, 744 F.2d 917 (2d Cir. 1984).

43. See amendment final judgment, para. 8, as set out in *Buffalo Broadcasting Co. v. American Soc'y of Composers, Authors & Publishers*, 546 F. Supp. 274, 278 (D.N.Y. 1982).

44. *Buffalo Broadcasting Co.*, 546 F. Supp., 279.

45. *Buffalo Broadcasting Co.*, 744 F.2d 917 (2d. Cir. 1984).

46. An astute program licensee might try to shift advertising revenue outside the base period to avoid paying royalties on some fraction of the revenues attributable to the music. This strategy will not, of course, help the blanket licensee, whose fees are tied to total broadcast revenue. Nor will it work if two or more program licenses cover adjacent periods; what is lost on the one is saved on the other. But the tactic could have some modest effect if the adjacent period uses no broadcast music. Yet some adjustment could be made to the base formula in the face of heavy advertisement revenues before or after the period covered by the program license.

47. *United States v. ASCAP* (In re Buffalo Broad. Co.), 1992–1994 Copyright L. Dec. (CCH) para. 27,088 (S.D.N.Y. 1993). For discussion, on which this account is based, see Einhorn, "Intellectual Property and Antitrust," 1, 11–13.

48. "ASCAP's blanket license for major radio stations is 1.615 percent of adjusted gross revenue. For program users, percentage fees per licensed program are set at 4.22 percent of the first 10 percent of weighted program hours where feature music is used. Fees for all additional hours with feature music are set at 2.135 percent. ASCAP then adds on additional 0.24 percent for a 'mini-blanket' to cover all music used on radio commercials. Depending on the number of weighted hours, the markup of the program percentage above the blanket rate may rate from 60 to 177 percent"; Einhorn, "Intellectual Property and Antitrust," 1, 13. At the last figure, the moment music broadcast exceeds about nine hours; it is cheaper to purchase the blanket license.

49. SAFJ, para. 8 (a), http://www.usdoj.gov/atr/cases/f6300/6396.pdf (accessed November 7, 2005).

50. Einhorn, "Intellectual Property and Antitrust," 14–15.

51. *United States v. United Shoe Machinery Corp.*, 391 U.S. 244 (1968).

52. Hovenkamp, *The Antitrust Enterprise* (describing the *United Shoe* decree as "poorly structured"); and Robert W. Crandall, *Costly Exercises in Futility: Breaking Up Firms to Increase Competition* 7, AEI-Brookings Joint Center Related Publication 03-32 (December 2003), http://www.aei.brookings.org/publications/abstract.php?pid=408 (accessed November 21, 2006). Crandall notes that "there is no evidence that its dismemberment increased competition in shoe machinery."

53. *United Shoe Corp.*, 247 U.S., 45, quoting Justice Holmes's decision in *Winslow*, 202 U.S., 217.

54. *United States v. United Shoe Machinery Co.*, 222 F. 349, 365 (D. Mass.).

55. U.S. Department of Justice and U.S. Federal Trade Commission, *Antitrust Guidelines for the Licensing of Intellectual Property*, April 6, 1995, http://www.usdoj.gov/atr/public/guidelines/0558.pdf (accessed April 6, 2006). For discussion, see Richard A. Epstein, *Intellectual Property for the Technological Age*, May 2006, 15–16, http://www.nam.org/s_nam/bin.asp?CID=202515&DID=236749&DOC=FILE.PDF (accessed November 7, 2006).

56. http://www.aei.brookings.org/publications/abstract.php?pid=408 *United Shoe Corp.*, 247 U.S., 51.

57. Ibid., 45–47.

58. Ibid., 59–60.

59. Ibid., 61.

60. Ibid., 70–71 (Day, J., dissenting).

61. Ibid., 64.

62. Ibid., 65.

63. *United Shoe Machinery Corp. v. United States*, 258 U.S. 451, 456–57 (1922). The invalidated terms included:

(1) the restricted use clause, which provides that the leased machinery shall not, nor shall any part thereof, be used upon shoes, etc., or portions, thereof, upon which certain other operations have not been performed on other machines of the defendants; (2) the exclusive use clause, which provides that if the lessee fails to use exclusively machinery of certain kinds made by the lessor, the lessor shall have the right to cancel the right to use all such machinery so leased; (3) the supplies clause, which provides that the lessee shall purchase supplies exclusively from the lessor; (4) the patent insole clause, which provides that the lessee shall only use machinery leased on shoes which have had certain other operations performed upon them by the defendants' machines; (5) the additional machinery clause, which provides that the lessee shall take all additional machinery for certain kinds of work from the lessor or lose his right to retain the machines which he has already leased; (6) the factory output clause, which requires the payment of a royalty on shoes operated upon by machines made by competitors; (7) the discriminatory royalty clause, providing lower royalty for lessees who agree not to use certain machinery on shoes lasted on machines other than those leased from the lessor.

64. Ibid., 458–60, citing *Cromwell v. County of Sac*, 94 U.S. 351 (1877). In modern law, changes in legal theories generally do not preclude the application of res judicata, for otherwise no claim would ever be settled given the constant transformation of the law. The modern test asks whether the two disputes arise out of the same set of operative facts, which they surely did.

65. Ibid., 463.

66. For the modern contrast, compare *Kaiser Aetna v. United States*, 444 U.S. 164 (1979), and *Loretto v. TelePrompter*, 458 U.S. 419 (1982), both of which give powerful protection of the rights of exclusive use of tangible property, with *Penn Central v. City of New York*, 438 U.S. 104 (1978), which offers much weaker protection for the rights to use and dispose of property. That two-part view has carried over to intellectual property rights more generally. See *Monsanto Inc. v. Ruckleshaus*, 467 U.S. 986, 1000–02 (1984) dealing with the protection of trade secrets subject to the regulatory process. I have critiqued these developments in Richard A. Epstein, "The Constitutional Protection of Trade Secrets under the Takings Clause," *University of Chicago Law Review* 71 (Winter 2004): 57–73.

67. For the obvious crosscurrents on this point, see *E. Bement & Sons v. National Harrow Co.*, 186 U.S. 70 (1902) (sustaining contract provision that voided license if too few licenses were issued).

68. *United States v. United Shoe Machinery Corp.*, 110 F. Supp. 295, 298 (1953).

69. *United Shoe Machinery Corp. v. United States*, 347 U.S. 521 (1954). The entire opinion reads: "The case having been fully argued and the Court being satisfied that the findings are justified by the evidence and support the decree, the judgment is affirmed."

70. 110 F. Supp., 339.

71. Ibid., 329–33.

72. Ibid., 312.

73. Ibid., 319.

74. Ibid., 348.

75. Only the full-capacity clause might have some restrictive effect, but even there it is hard to see why a firm would *not* want to use a machine to its full capacity even in the absence of the clause.

76. 110 F. Supp., 352.

77. Ibid., 349.

78. Ibid., 344.

79. Ibid., 351.

80. On these dangers, see Epstein, *Intellectual Property for the Technological Age*, 16–17.

81. *United Shoe Machinery Corp.*, 391 U.S., 246.

82. Ibid., 251.

83. *United States v. United Shoe Machinery Corp.*, 1969 Trade Cas. (CCH) P. 72,688, para. 6.

84. Crandall, *Costly Exercises in Futility*, 5n83.

85. See Phillipe Aghion and Patrick Bolton, "Contracts as a Barrier to Entry," *American Economic Review* 77, no. 3 (June 1987): 388–401; Joseph F. Brodley and Ching-to Albert Ma, "Contract Penalties, Monopolizing Strategies, and Antitrust Policy," *Stanford Law Review* 45, no. 5 (May 1993): 1161–1213.

86. See Scott E. Masten and Edward A. Snyder, "*United States Versus United Shoe Machinery Corporation*: On The Merits," *Journal of Law and Economics* 36, no.1 (April 1993): 33–70, explicitly acknowledging the arguments of Aghion and Bolton, "Contracts as a Barrier to Entry," 34.

87. *United States v. Aluminum Co. of America*, 148 F.2d 416, 430 (2d Cir. 1945).

Chapter 3: The Breakup of the Bell System

1. Peter W. Huber, Michael K. Kellogg, and John Thorne, *Federal Telecommunications Law*, 2d ed. (Frederick, Md.: Aspen Publishers, 1999), 353.

2. Ibid., 354.

3. See United States Complaint, in *United States v. Western Electr. Co.*, Civil Action No. 17-49 (D.N.J. January 14, 1949), reproduced in Huber, Kellogg, and Thorne, *Federal Telecommunications Law*, 1999 ed., 35n115.

4. See Richard Schmalensee, "Bill Baxter in the Antitrust Arena: An Economist's Appreciation," *Stanford Law Review* 51 (May 1999): 1317–32, 1325–26.

5. *AT&T*, 552 F. Supp., 188–91.

6. Ibid., 191–95. Judge Greene lifted proposed restrictions on the BOCs to provide customer premises equipment or directory advertising (Yellow Pages),

finding that neither of these activities posed any real danger of abusing their monopoly position.

7. Lawrence A. Sullivan and Ellen Hertz, "The AT&T Antitrust Consent Decree: Should Congress Change the Rules," *Berkeley Technology Law Journal* 5, no. 2 (Fall 1990): 236.

8. Peter W. Huber, Michael K. Kellogg, and John Thorne, *Federal Telecommunications Law* (Boston, Mass: Little Brown, 1992), chapters 4–7, covering about two hundred pages of material. The same issues are covered in less space in Huber, Kellogg, and Thorne, *Federal Telecommunications Law*, 1999 ed.

9. *AT&T*, 552 F. Supp., 170.

10. *AT&T*, 552 F. Supp. 131, 154–56 (1982).

11. *Maryland v. United States*, 460 U.S., 1001–2 (1983).

12. *AT&T*, 552 F. Supp. 131, 157 (1982).

13. Ibid., 211–12.

14. Ibid., 232–33. One obvious AT&T advantage at the time concerned dialing parity. More digits were required to access long-distance through AT&T rivals than through AT&T.

15. *United States v. Western Electric Co.*, 569 F. Supp. 1057, 1123–24 (1983).

16. *Maryland v. United States*, 460 U.S., 1003–5.

17. Jerry A. Hausman, J. Gregory Sidak, and Hal J. Singer, "Residential Demand for Broadband Telecommunications and Consumer Access to Unaffiliated Internet Content Providers," *Yale Journal of Regulation* 18, no. 1 (Winter 2001): 129–73.

18. Paul W. MacIvoy and Kenneth Robinson, "Losing By Judicial Policymaking: The First Year of the AT&T Divestiture," *Yale Journal of Regulation* 2, no. 2 (Spring 1985): 227.

19. Ibid., 226.

20. *AT&T*, 552 F. Supp., 175–76.

21. Ibid., 162–63. At least from the famous *Hush-A-Phone* incident in the 1950s, Bell had objected that attaching a mechanical device—not dissimilar to cupping one's hands over one's ears—to an ordinary receiver violated the tariff that forbade "attachment to the telephone of any device 'not furnished by the telephone company.'" *Hush-A-Phone Corp. v. United States*, 238 F.2d 266, 267 (D.C. Cir. 1956), rejecting any claim of impairment.

22. Indeed the single greatest mistake under the Telecommunications Act of 1996 was its authorization of the forced sale of "unbundled network elements" (or UNEs) to new entrants into the market. The transactions costs for various portions of a switch are exceedingly high, and the FCC could never develop a coherent pricing system for the forced exchanges. See Richard A. Epstein, "Takings, Commons, and Associations: Why the Telecommunications Act of 1996 Misfired," *Yale Journal of Regulation* 22, no. 2 (Summer 2005): 315–48.

23. *AT&T*, 552 F. Supp., 164, citing *Alcoa*.

24. *AT&T*, 552 F. Supp., 165.

25. Ibid., 165n142.

26. *U.S. v. AT&T*, 552 F. Supp., 164. A judge's favorite writers reflect his intellectual orientation. Judge Greene took a dim view of Robert Bork and Philip Areeda, both of whom had little use for the populist arguments in favor of the antitrust laws; see 552 F. Supp, 164n139 explicitly rejecting the views of Robert H. Bork, *The Antitrust Paradox* (New York: The Free Press, 1978), 50–89; Philip Areeda and Donald Turner, *Antitrust Law*, section 103–12 (Boston, Mass: Little Brown, 1978). Instead he preferred the decidedly populist views of Arthur Schlesinger and Ralph Nader; 552 F. Supp., 165n141.

27. *AT&T*, 552 F. Supp., 165. At some points, Judge Greene suggested that only the new AT&T could spawn mischief. "To the extent, then, that the proposed decree proceeds on the assumption that the structural reorganization will make it impossible, or at least unprofitable, for AT&T to engage in anticompetitive practices, it is fully consistent with the public interest in the enforcement of the antitrust laws"; ibid., 167.

28. Ibid., 169n161. "Although the decree requires the Operating Companies to file 'cost justified' tariffs for access charges, it leaves to the regulators the decision as to what costs should be included within this calculation."

29. *AT&T*, 551 F. Supp., 172n72.

30. *AT&T*, 552 F. Supp. 231.

31. *United States v. Western Elec. Co.*, 569 F. Supp., 990, 1119 (D.D.C. 1983).

32. See Huber, Kellogg, and Thorne, *Federal Communications Law*, 1999 ed., 995, n. 119.

33. Ibid., 1005.

34. Ibid., 996.

35. Ibid., 997.

36. Huber, Kellogg, and Thorne, *Federal Communications Law*, 1999 ed., note 119.

37. *United States v. Western Electric*, 1989 U.S. Dist. Lexis 8646. For discussion see Huber, Kellogg, and Thorne, *Federal Telecommunications Law*, 1992 ed., section 4.10, 291, 293–94.

38. Huber, Kellogg, and Thorne, *Federal Telecommunications Law*, 1992 ed., 301. Judge Greene did lift the restrictions for customer premises equipment, which the BOCs had previously been allowed to provide but not to manufacture. Those activities were a step further removed from the telecommunications grid.

39. Ibid., 292.

40. Huber, Kellogg, and Thorne, *Federal Telecommunications Law*, 1992 ed., 378.

41. Epstein, "Takings, Commons, and Associations," 315.

Chapter 4: Microsoft

1. *United States v. Terminal R R Ass'n*, 224 US 383 (1912). In modern terms, the elements of that doctrine are:

(1) control of the essential facility by a monopolist; (2) a competitor's inability practically or reasonably to duplicate the essential facility; (3) the denial of the use of the facility to a competitor; and (4) the feasibility of providing the facility to competitors; *MCI Communications, Inc. v. Amer. Tel. & Tel. Co.*, 708 F.2d 1081, 1132–33 (7th Cir. 1982).

2. The literature on this subject has become exhaustive. See the fundamental contribution in William F. Baxter, "Bank Interchange of Transactional Paper: Legal and Economic Perspectives," *Journal of Law and Economics* 26, no. 3 (October 1983): 541–88. For an informative account of the payment industry, see David S. Evans and Richard Schmalensee, *Paying with Plastic* (Cambridge, Mass.: MIT Press, 2003). For some recent works on the subject, with emphasis on credit cards, see, for example, Timothy Muris, "Payment Card Regulation and the (Mis)Application of the Economics of Two-Sided Markets," *Columbia Business Law Review* 2005, no. 3 (2005): 515–50; Robert Litan and Alex J. Pollock, "The Future of Charge Card Networks," AEI Brookings Joint Institute Working Paper, February 2006, on file with author. For my own contribution on this subject, see Richard A. Epstein, "The Regulation of Interchange Fees: Australian Fine-Tuning Gone Awry," *Columbia Business Law Review* 2005, no. 3 (2005): 551–97. See also Dennis W. Carlton and Alan S. Frankel, "The Antitrust Economics of Credit Card Networks," *Antitrust Law Journal* 63, no. 2 (1995): 643; Lloyd Constantine, Jeffrey I. Shinder, and Kerin E. Couglin, "In Re Visa Check/MasterMoney Antitrust Litigation: A Study of Market Failure in a Two-Sided Market," *Columbia Business Law Review* 2005, no. 3 (2005): 599–614; Dennis W. Carlton and Alan Frankel, "Transaction Costs, Externalities and Two-Sided Payment Markets," *Columbia Business Law Review* 2005, no. 3 (2005): 617–42.

3. Senate Banking Committee, Subcommittee on Financial Institutions, *Hearing on Competition and Innovation in the Credit Card Industry at the Consumer and Network Level*, testimony of Phillip Purcell (chairman and CEO of Morgan Stanley Dean Witter), May 25, 2000, 106th Cong., http://banking.senate.gov/00_05hrg/052500/purcell.htm (accessed December 11, 2006). One instructive exception is the Discover Card system, which started with a large base of Sears customers and sets lower fees for merchants in order to lure them into its system.

4. See declaration of Kenneth J. Arrow, January 17, 1995, submitted in *United States v. Microsoft Corp.*, No. 94-1564 (D.D.C. 1994), 1452.

5. This was also the Arrow conclusion, ibid., 1453–54. For similar discussions on the antitrust laws, see Muris, "Payment Card Regulation," and Epstein, "The Regulation of Interchange Fees."

6. Hovenkamp, *The Antitrust Enterprise*, 267.

7. *United States v. Microsoft Corporation*, 56 F.3d 1448, 1452 (D.C. Cir. 1995). "The government did not allege and does not contend—and this is of crucial significance to this case—that Microsoft obtained its alleged monopoly position in violation of the antitrust laws." The court of appeals rebuked the district court judge for acting as

though illegality was a given in the case. "The complaint did not allege—because the government did not believe it was true—that Microsoft's dominant market position resulted from illegal means. The district court and amici would have it be otherwise, but neither have the power to force the government to make that claim." Ibid., 1460.

8. Ibid., 1451–52.

9. *United States v. Microsoft Corp.*, 159 F.R.D. 318 (D.C. D.C. 1995).

10. See 159 F.R.D., 332.

11. James Wallace and Jim Erickson, *Hard Drive: Bill Gates and the Making of the Microsoft Empire* (New York: HarperCollins, 1992).

12. See *United States v. Microsoft*, 56 F.3d, 1463 (colloquy with Bingaman). Product delays after introduction are, of course, common, and the illegality of this practice has by no means been established. The legal issues were not resolved in this case because Microsoft denied the charge, and the government refused to prosecute for insufficient evidence.

13. Ibid.

14. Ibid., 1459.

15. *Triennial Review Opinion*, 900 F.2d 283, 309 (D.C. Cir. 1990) (emphasis in original), quoting earlier cases.

16. The government had initially asked for a version of the operating system that did not contain any browser—that is, a system with no icon or menu entry that allowed access to the Internet Explorer. The government did not prevail on that demand.

17. For a discussion, see David A. Heiner, "Assessing Tying Claims in the Context of Software Integration: A Suggested Framework for Applying the Rule of Reason Analysis," *University of Chicago Law Review* 72, no. 1 (Winter 2005): 125–26.

18. *Telex Corp. v. International Business Machines Corp.*, 367 F. 258, 347 (D. Okla. 1973).

19. Ibid.

20. See *United States v. Armour & Co.*, 402 U.S. 673, 681–82 (1971).

21. On appeal, Justice Williams summarized Microsoft's argument as follows: "Microsoft stresses § IV(E)(i)'s 'integrated products' proviso, saying that the addition of any feature to an operating system, as by simply putting the disk containing a compatible application in the same box with the operating system disk and requiring an OEM to install both, creates an integrated product—unless Microsoft also licenses the feature on a stand-alone basis 'in the OEM channel.'" 147 F.3d, 947–48. In effect this reading makes the proviso elective, because an integrated product does not lose that status if it is distributed separately in downloaded form.

22. *United States v. Microsoft*, 147 F.3d, 935, 949–50 (D.C. 1998).

23. *United States v. Microsoft*, 147 F.3d, 948.

24. In order listed, New York, California, Connecticut, Florida, Illinois, Iowa, Kansas, Kentucky, Louisiana, Maryland, Massachusetts, Michigan, Minnesota, New Mexico, North Carolina, Ohio, South Carolina, Utah, West Virginia, Wisconsin, and the District of Columbia.

25. *United States v. Microsoft,* and *State of New York v. Microsoft,* 87 F.Supp.2d 30 (D.C. D.C. 2000).

26. *United States v. Microsoft,* and *State of New York v. Microsoft,* 97 F. Supp.2d 59 (D.C. D.C. 2000).

27. *United States v. Microsoft Corp.,* 253 F.3d 34 (D.C. Cir. 2001).

28. *United States v. Microsoft,* 253 F.3d, 51–58.

29. See Heiner, 126–29, for a lucid discussion.

30. *United States v. Microsoft,* 253 F.3d, 53.

31. The phrase dates at least from Philip E. Areeda and Donald F. Turner, *Antitrust Law* 3, para. 626g(3), 83, discussed in Herbert Hovenkamp, "Exclusion and the Sherman Act," *University of Chicago Law Review* 72, no. 1 (2005): 149. For an alternative definition that defines exclusive practices in terms of the ability to exclude an equally efficient rival, see Richard A. Posner, *Antitrust Law,* 2d ed. (Chicago: University of Chicago Press, 2001), 194–95. None of these tests quite does the job, but a detailed critique lies beyond the scope of this essay.

32. 253 F.3d, 61.

33. Ibid., 58–59. As the Federal Circuit succinctly stated: "Intellectual property rights do not confer a privilege to violate the antitrust laws." *In re Indep. Serv. Orgs. Antitrust Litig.,* 203 F.3d 1322, 1325 (Fed. Cir. 2000).

34. 253 F.3d, 64–65.

35. Ibid., 65.

36. Ibid., 67, quoting the findings of Judge Jackson below.

37. Ibid., 68.

38. Ibid., 70–72 (Apple), and 79 (Intel). Section 1 makes it generally illegal for unrelated firms to enter into any agreement by which they collectively refuse to deal with outsiders. The dominant firm is subject to a parallel restraint.

39. 253 F.3d, 95–97.

40. For some sense of these problems, see testimony of Kevin M. Murphy, Civil Action No. 98-1233, April 12, 2002, 15–63.

41. Ibid., 19–23.

42. Ibid., 54–58.

43. *Microsoft II,* 253 F.3d, 78–80, noting the lower standard of proof in injunctive relief cases.

44. Hovenkamp, *The Antitrust Enterprise,* 301.

45. *Microsoft II,* 253 F.3d, 103.

46. The quotation marks are meant to suggest that in some cases the extraction game makes social sense. The patent owner that is able to price-discriminate serves two social functions. First, price discrimination allows the invention to reach customers who value the patented invention at above the competitive (license, say) price but below the monopoly one. A single price keeps those individuals out of the market. Second, price discrimination increases patent yield and thus creates an incentive for the earlier development of the patented device. This point restates an earlier

observation: Strong exclusive-dealing arrangements have the virtue of bringing new advances in operating systems more quickly to market.

47. See Hovenkamp, *The Antitrust Enterprise*, 191–98, and sources cited therein. See 343–44 for a discussion of the anticompetitive effects of the act.

48. 2002 Microsoft Consent Decree, III(D).

49. See Heiner, "Assessing Tying Claims," 128: "Software developers call upon underlying platform software to obtain basic system services utilized by applications generally rather than having to recreate such functionality themselves in their own applications." These include the ability to resort to common icons, toolbars, dropdown menus, and the like; ibid., 128. That standardization further helps consumers as well.

50. 2002 Microsoft Consent Decree, III(I)(2).

51. Article 82 of the Treaty Establishing the European Community (ex article 86):

> Any abuse by one or more undertakings of a dominant position within the common market or in a substantial part of it shall be prohibited as incompatible with the common market insofar as it may affect trade between Member States.

> Such abuse may, in particular, consist in:

> (a) directly or indirectly imposing unfair purchase or selling prices or other unfair trading conditions;
> (b) limiting production, markets or technical development to the prejudice of consumers;
> (c) applying dissimilar conditions to equivalent transactions with other trading parties, thereby placing them at a competitive disadvantage;
> (d) making the conclusion of contracts subject to acceptance by the other parties of supplementary obligations which, by their nature or according to commercial usage, have no connection with the subject of such contracts.

52. Decision of the European Commission, March 25, 2004 (Case COMP/C-3/37.792 Microsoft).

53. *Kewanee Oil Co. v. Bicron Corp.*, 416 U.S. 470 (1974). There is, in fact, no reason to limit trade-secret protection to patentable secrets when the consequences of the two forms of intellectual property are so different. The successful registration of a patent excludes everyone within the jurisdiction from making use of the invention, even if they made an independent discovery of it. But trade secrets are not protected from any form of independent invention at all, and thus do not have the same preclusive effect.

54. Joint Status Report on Microsoft's Compliance with the Final Judgments, *U.S. v. Microsoft Corp.*, Civil Action No. 98–1232, 4–5.

55. For discussion, see Michael DeBow, "State Antitrust Enforcement: Empirical Evidence and a Modest Reform Proposal," in *Competition Laws in Conflict: Antitrust*

Jurisdiction in the Global Economy, ed. Richard A. Epstein and Michael Greve (Washington, D.C.: The AEI Press, 2004). According to Richard A. Posner, "Enforcement by State Attorney Generals," in *Competition Laws in Conflict*, 252, 358, "The use of the antitrust laws to harass competitors is an old story but a true one, and given the political incentives of state attorneys general, the risk is great that in deciding whether to bring an antitrust suit against a competitor of a resident enterprise a state attorney general will not be scrupulous in the exercise of his enforcement discretion and will bring and press the suit even if unconvinced of its merits. This is a form of protectionism."

56. *Massachusetts v. Microsoft*, 373 F.3d 1199 (D.C. Cir. 2004).

57. Hovenkamp, *The Antitrust Enterprise*, quoting from *Microsoft III*.

58. Ibid., 298.

59. Ibid., 292–93.

60. Ibid., 300.

61. Eliot Spitzer, et al., Joint Status Report on Microsoft's Compliance with the Final Judgments, submitted to U.S. Department of Justice, Antitrust Division, February 8, 2006.

62. Hovenkamp, *The Antitrust Enterprise*, 299.

63. University of Illinois at Urbana-Champaign, *Browser Market Shares*, data at http://www.ews.uiuc.edu/bstats/ (accessed November 28, 2006). This study is based on hits on home pages of undergraduate engineering majors at UIUC campus, which is not exactly a random study.

64. Ibid.

65. Hovenkamp, *The Antitrust Enterprise*, 299.

66. Testimony of John Soyring (IBM director of network computing software services) in *United States v. Microsoft*, November 17, 1998.

67. Hovenkamp, *The Antitrust Enterprise*, 297.

68. Ibid., 294.

69. I was a great fan of my nimble Microsoft Word 5.0 software for Mac even after the publication of the balky Windows 98. But I eagerly abandoned it as the upgrades came out, which allowed me to receive and work on documents sent by others that had been prepared by more modern programs.

70. Hovenkamp, *The Antitrust Enterprise*, 298–99. See also *New York v. Microsoft*, 224 F.Supp.2d, 157.

71. 224 F.Supp.2d, 158, affirmed on this point in *Microsoft IV*, 373 F.3d 1199.

72. Hovenkamp, *The Antitrust Enterprise*, 301.

73. 224 F. Supp. 2d, 252, quoted in *Microsoft IV*, 373 F.3d, 1210.

74. *Microsoft IV*, 373 F.3d, 1210.

75. See Hovenkamp, *The Antitrust Enterprise*, 302.

76. Hovenkamp, *The Antitrust Enterprise*, 299–300.

77. Microsoft Corporation, "Microsoft Windows Principles: Twelve Tenets for Encouraging Innovation and Competition in the Microsoft Ecosystem," July 2006,

http://www.microsoft.com/presspass/newsroom/winxp/WindowsPrinciples.mspx (accessed November 9, 2006).

78. Ibid. (italics in original).

79. *U.S. v. Microsoft Corp.*, Civil Action No. 98-1232 (CKK) (D.C.C. 2002), http://www.usdoj.gov/atr/cases/f9400/9495.htm (accessed November 9, 2006).

80. Thus from the Joint Status Report on Microsoft's Compliance with Final Judgment on June 1, 2005:

> III, UPDATE ON MICROSOFT'S COMPLIANCE WITH THE FINAL JUDGMENTS
>
> Microsoft continues to make full compliance with its obligations under the Final Judgments an important priority throughout the company, and devotes substantial resources to its compliance work. While issues inevitably will arise, Microsoft has worked diligently and cooperatively to respond to and resolve all inquiries from Plaintiffs. Microsoft believes that Plaintiffs' section of this report adequately reflects this cooperation and the continued commitment of Microsoft to comply fully with the Final Judgments and to go even further in a spirit of accommodation; Eliot Spitzer et al., Joint Status Report on Microsoft's Compliance with Final Judgment (June 1, 2005), http://www.usdoj.gov/atr/cases/f209300/209307.htm (accessed December 11, 2006).

Identical language appears in the October 2005 report at http://www.usdoj.gov/atr/cases/f212100/212195.htm (accessed December 11, 2006), which also said that some twenty-five complaints had been filed against Microsoft since January 25, 2005, of which twenty-four were without merit and the last was resolved by the passage of events; ibid., II B.

81. See Michelle Bailey, Vernon Turner, Jean Bozman, and Janet Waxman, *Bulletin: Linux Servers: What's the Hype, and What's the Reality*, IDC Bulletin #21610 (March 2000), 4.

82. This backward user has two different email systems (neither Microsoft products) and two browsers (one of which, less used, is IE).

Chapter 5: Lessons Learned

1. For one recent demonstration of the point, see Jim Powell, *Bully Boy: The Truth about Theodore Roosevelt's Legacy* (New York: Crown Forum, 2006).

2. See, respectively, American Bar Association Antitrust Section, *Antitrust Law Developments*, 5th ed. (Chicago: American Bar Association, 2002), 758n217 and accompanying text, and 763n254.

About the Author

Richard A. Epstein is the James Parker Hall Distinguished Service Professor of Law at the University of Chicago Law School, where he has taught since 1972. Since 2000, he has been the Peter and Kirstin Bedford Senior Fellow at the Hoover Institution. Professor Epstein has been a member of the American Academy of Arts and Sciences since 1985, and a senior fellow at the Center for Clinical Medical Ethics at the University of Chicago Medical School since 1983. He has edited the *Journal of Legal Studies* and the *Journal of Law and Economics*, and at present, he is a director of the John M. Olin Program in Law and Economics. He is the author most recently of *Overdose: How Excessive Government Regulation Stifles Pharmaceutical Innovation* (Yale University Press, 2006), and *How Progressives Rewrote the Constitution* (Cato Institute, 2006). His earlier books include *Skepticism and Freedom: A Modern Case for Classical Liberalism* (University of Chicago Press, 2003); *Simple Rules for a Complex World* (Harvard University Press, 1995), and *Takings: Private Property and the Power of Eminent Domain* (Harvard University Press, 1985).

Index

and Swift & Co., 25–29
and United Shoe case, 40–42, 45,
49, 50–52
Swift and Co., 18
antitrust action against, 22
attempts to modify decree later,
25–28
consent decree, description, 22–25,
117
effects of decree, 28–29
Swift standard, 7–8, 29, 48, 51, 72

Telecommunications Act (1996), 58,
64, 73, 105–6
Television and ASCAP/BMI saga,
34–39
Thorne, John, 58, 70
Torrington, 118
Trade secrets, 79, 99–100
Truman administration, 55
Tunney Act, 5, 66, 72, 80–81
Two-sided market principle, 75–76

United Artists, 20
United Fruit, 119
United Shoe Machinery Company
cases, 18, 76, 78, 105, 118
decennial review, 50–53
first round of litigation and consent
decree, 40–43
second round, 43–44
third round, 44–50

*United States v. Aluminum Company of
America*, 20
See Alcoa, Aluminum Company of
America
United States v. ASCAP, 35
See American Society of Composers,
Authors, and Publishers
United States v. Microsoft, 7
See Microsoft entries
United States v. Paramount Pictures Inc., 20
See Paramount Pictures
United States v. Swift & Co., 22
See Swift & Co.
United States v. United Shoe Corporation
(1918), 40
See United Shoe Machinery Company
United States v. Winslow (1913), 40
Universal, 20
Unix system, 85, 91

Vista Operating System, 108

Waste Management of Georgia Inc.
et al., 120
Western Electric, 55, 66
Williams, Stephen F., 83–84
Willis-Graham Act, 55
Wilson Administration, 22, 54
Windows, 81–83, 85–90, 98–99,
102–3, 104
Winston, Clifford, 18, 19, 20
Wyzanski, Charles E., 45–52